I'M KEEPING YOUNG

The Everyday Life of an MP

GEORGE YOUNG

© George Young 2015

Published by George Young

A CIP catalogue record for this book is available from the British Library.

ISBN 978-0-9934257-0-7

Every effort has been made to trace the copyright owner of the illustrations in the book and the author apologises for any omissions

Cover illustration by Doug Ensom

Acknowledgements to Aquascutum for the cartoon

Printed in the UK by York Publishing Services Ltd

Contents

Part 1

(From leaving the Government in 1986 to rejoining it in 1990)

Part 2

(Ministerial career under John Major)

Part 3

(Years in Opposition)

Part 4

(In David Cameron's Cabinet)

List of Illustrations

"Hallelujah! A friend's book that I can unreservedly recommend! That Sir George Young MP had a rather brilliant sideline as a columnist for his local paper was an open secret in a House where many attempt this but few succeed. Young does, triumphantly. Light-hearted, sharp-witted, guaranteed to draw a smile, and often a snort of laughter, these pieces reveal a politician who is also a human being. Young has wisdom, mercy and humour, but above all a knack for lucid storytelling. His modesty of tone cloaks a mordant wit. This is a bedside book, each essay a little gem, to be dipped into time and again. Whatever else may be said about Sir George Young's career in politics, it was a loss to journalism."

MATTHEW PARRIS

Foreword

I was elected to the House of Commons in February 1974 and retired from it in 2015. I am grateful to the electorate of Ealing Acton and North West Hampshire for their patience. Roughly half my time was on my Party's Front Bench and half on the backbenches, depending on how much of an irritant I was when freed of collective responsibility; and how much value I was able to add when in Government. My portfolios covered health, housing, planning, tax, transport and, finally, I was what is referred to as a "Usual Channel."

We had three young children when first elected, with a fourth joining us in 1975. Those early years, with a majority in Acton of 808, all night sittings, and a Government with a precarious majority were politically exciting, but domestically disruptive. Domesticity was further challenged by the arrival of red boxes in 1979 when my Party won and I was made a Minister. Relative serenity was established in 1986, when Margaret Thatcher returned me to the backbenches, leaving me free to oppose the Poll Tax.

I then wrote some articles for the Guardian. The Editor of my local paper, the Ealing and Acton Gazette, thought he detected some literary potential and asked me to write a weekly column. There was mutual agreement that it would not be party political. It suited him because, had it become so, the two other MPs in the borough would have demanded equal space and the appetite for a political diet amongst his readers was small. It suited me because I took the view that my voters knew I was a politician, but they weren't sure I was a human being.

I wrote the column until 1990, when I rejoined the Government. The Ministerial rules prevented me continuing to write, so my wife Aurelia took it over. (See Page 55.) It stopped in 1995 because the column was scoured by gossip columnists looking for salacious titbits about Cabinet Ministers and their families, and we could do without the hassle.

In 1997, after the abolition of my Ealing Acton constituency and my Party's loss of office, I migrated to North West Hampshire. The Editor of the Andover Advertiser generously extended his hospitality to my column, where it appeared fortnightly from the end of 1999 until October 2012. My appointment as Government Chief Whip, operating below the radar, meant that my media profile should be minimal and, as in 1995, the media were beginning to rifle through my literary dustbin and publish titbits. The book ends with some pieces I wrote when I was Chief Whip that were never published and a handful of pieces I wrote after I left office for the fourth time in 2014, and returned to the Backbenches.

This is a collection from these columns, with acknowledgements to the papers in which they originally appeared and with a few changes to make them intelligible to today's reader. They do not pretend to be profound pieces; they were written to give an insight into the challenges of bringing up a family whose breadwinner was in the House of Commons and, at times, in the Government.

I am grateful to Aurelia and our four children who appeared regularly in these columns and bore the comments with fortitude; to Eleo Carson for her advice on preparing them for publication and to Paul and Gary at Bulpitts in Andover for their technical advice.

George Young
October 2015

.

Part 1

(From leaving the Government in 1986 to rejoining it
in 1990)

Deals on Wheels

August 1986

As the Government's privatisation programme gathers momentum with the imminent sale of British Gas, I can reveal the identity of the Government's first – and smallest – privatisation.

Not Amersham International, not National Freight, but the House of Commons Bicycle Pool.

Having arrived at Westminster in 1974 after a closely fought election, I applied for another elected office; that of Chairman of the All Party Friends of Cycling, a group that had been free-wheeling, if not free-loading, for some time with little agitation for a squarer deal for cyclists. This time, there were no other candidates and I was duly installed. My mission was to transform the view of MPs towards cycling, and then, with their support, to transform the view of the nation – so that MPs who cycled to work were no longer considered eccentric.

I wrote to all the bicycle manufacturers and asked them to sponsor a bicycle for a new House Of Commons Bicycle Pool, having first got the consent of the then Speaker, Selwyn Lloyd, for this enterprise. There was a good response, and a large fleet was soon at my disposal.

I then wrote to my 629 colleagues, telling them that, for £5 a year to cover maintenance costs, they could borrow a bicycle from the pool whenever they wanted. We were in business; MPs who hadn't cycled since they did newspaper delivery rounds took to two wheels, fanned out from Westminster. Horizons were broadened and waistlines narrowed.

And then the problems began. My colleagues sometimes went out to lunch on a bicycle, but, for reasons that can only be guessed at, returned to the House by taxi. My bicycles were abandoned outside the choicest restaurants and nightclubs, and had to be tracked down and retrieved. Some MPs took the bicycles back to their constituencies and they (the bicycles) were never seen again. The batteries from the lights were borrowed for portable radios and never returned.

We kept the show on the road with some difficulty until the 1979 General Election, when I became a Minister and so precluded from office with the All Party Friends of Cycling. No other volunteer to run the pool could be found. We had an emergency meeting, invited sealed bids for the assets and sold the fleet to the regular members of the pool. Privatisation has not looked back since.

Taxi!

September 1986

Readers have asked me to confirm reports in Another Newspaper that British Rail refunded me £125 when they recently let me down.

They are true, but before Ealing commuters contact their MP to enlist his or her support for their own claims, the circumstances were unusual.

I was due, as Minister for Housing, to open a sheltered housing scheme in Barnstaple. Trains don't go to Barnstaple anymore, but it seemed sensible to catch the train to Taunton and then entrust myself to the Government Car Service for the final lap.

To catch the train to Taunton, I first had to catch a feeder train from Maidenhead to Reading. That was cancelled, and the Taunton train pulled out of Reading station on time, four minutes before I arrived. The next Taunton train would have been too late.

I jumped into a taxi outside Reading station "Take me to Barnstaple!" I cried. "Is that Swindon way?" asked the driver. I said it was, and waited until he was on the M4 before revealing the full extent of his commitment.

He took it philosophically. Two problems then became apparent. One was his, and the other was mine. His problem was that his meter would not go beyond £99.99, being calibrated to take folk from Reading Station to Battle Hospital. My problem was that my wallet wouldn't take me beyond Bristol.

I negotiated a fixed price contract, and rang my private secretary and told him to get £125 out of a hole in the wall in Barnstaple. The good fellow obliged and, when we arrived, he handed me an envelope with the speech and the driver an envelope with the money. The driver might have been hoping that this transaction might go unrecorded, but the insistence of the Accounting Officer at the Department of the

Environment for a receipt for every item of Ministerial expenditure put paid to that.

I thanked the driver for his co-operation and asked if there was anything I could do for him. He looked at the large crowd that had gathered outside the sheltered scheme.

"When you've cut the ribbon, guv, could you ask if there's anyone here who wants to go to Reading?"

***

The Sack

October 3 1986 (Guardian article)

In May 1979, the day after the General Election, No. 10 rang summoning me to Downing Street. Minutes later, the appointment to accept a Cabinet post was cancelled. They wanted the Hon George Younger, not Sir George Young. And an infinitely better Secretary of State for Scotland he turned out to be than the Member for Ealing Acton. My summons came two days later, for a humbler post. Seven years later, responding to a summons to the same destination, but with a different purpose, I wondered if by chance the No. 10 switchboard had got it wrong again, and the career of the present Secretary of State for Defence was drawing to a close. But it was not to be.

Last year, the pundits had tipped me for the sack and I survived. This year, they tipped me for promotion, and I was sacked. Any lingering doubts about the purpose of my visit were removed by the look on the face of the PM's Private Secretary, as he blindfolded me and led me up the stairs.

After the meeting, I walked across Parliament Street, unlocked my bicycle from the railings of the Banqueting Hall and cycled back to the Department. The will to live that enables London's cyclists to survive was momentarily dampened. Somewhere along my route, I was spotted by a carnivorous reporter from the Daily Mail hovering around Downing Street. He informed his readers the next day that, so swift is the transition from office, the Ministerial car which had transported me that morning had been summarily withdrawn and I was dependent on my own resources to get back to the Department to assemble my belongings.

A more reflective reporter, such as the ones who work for this paper, might have asked - if that was indeed the case - what was my bicycle doing chained to the Banqueting Hall opposite Downing Street?

On the eve of each reshuffle, rumoured and actual, did I wheel the machine up Parliament Street and secure it there, just in case I might need it the next day? Or perhaps it was there because I had gone there on it. Never mind; I'm sure Daily Mail readers will have worked it out for themselves.

Back in the Department, the formalities were exchanged with Private Office. I handed over the key to the red boxes, the card which operates the car-park barrier at 2 Marsham Street, the keys to my Ministerial room at the House and a cannon-ball which had been presented to me by a grateful Community Association in South London.

They handed over £8.12, being the balance of the Ministerial float, a highly ornate No Smoking sign, and a list of the 123 Adjournment Debates I had answered. (This, I am assured, is a record. Every previous Parliamentary Under-Secretary had displayed the characteristics that secure promotion or dismissal far earlier than me and had not done half that number.)

Farewells were exchanged with my Private Office, and I was relieved to notice the occasional tear glistening on the cheek. Waiting for the lift, I began to wonder what I should say to my wife.

I then realised I lacked two vital commodities. A diary and a car.

The first proved more difficult to find than the second. For the past seven years, my socio-political engagements had been handled by a diary secretary of impeccable efficiency and discretion. Her job was to conceal from numerous enquirers my availability on a given day until she had discovered whether it was an engagement I was likely to want to accept. Diaries for 1986 were no longer on sale in September.

Then the car. The vehicle which I have been using for weekend constituency work, which I thought was mine, turns out to be my wife's. Two other somewhat less attractive cars, which I distinctly recall paying for, turned out to belong to Son No. 1 and Daughter No. 1 respectively, whose academic careers at Oxford would apparently be irrevocably damaged without wheels.

Fortunately, one of the advantages of membership of the Acton Conservative Club is that it is rich in second hand car dealers, whose commitment to the Party has never been in doubt. After a traditional tyre-kicking dance in the car-park, £700 changed hands at the bar, and I was the proud owner of a seven year old Renault.

Then there were the bids from the media to comment on my dismissal. One of the advantages of leaving the Government after seven years, instead of after one, is that I have had the opportunity to observe colleagues' behaviour on the loss of their office. (And very many opportunities have there been.)

If interviewed, I could either have defended the Administration. Or I could have defended myself. For the past seven years, there had been a convenient community of interest, but that was no longer the case. Defending the Administration would have conceded the case for dismissal; defending myself would have criticised the Administration.

Although it is a subject on which I have views, I felt it best not to share them with an anxious nation.

But there are compensations; the loss of the Ministerial salary means that the Labour Party no longer regard me as well-off. And no more late night Adjournment Debates.

***

Teenage Party

October 1986

I had just had one of my less productive conversations with Son No. 2. I had spotted him leaving home, smelling of my aftershave and with a four-pack of Carlsberg taken from the fridge clumsily hidden under his jacket.

"Where are you going?" "Out"

"When will you be back?" "Late"

"How will you get back?" "Walk"

With that he disappeared into the night, with a headphone clamped over each ear.

I was woken up at 2am by the telephone.

"Dad?" "Yes"

"It's raining" "You woke me up to tell me about the weather?"

"It'll ruin my new shoes."

I dressed and drove to the house he was at.

Then came the sting.

"Can you drop off my mates on the way back?"

This was the cue for a number of dishevelled teenagers, too sensible to have rung their own parents, to emerge from hiding and get into the Volvo estate.

I remembered the routine from the older children. You look each passenger in the face, work out which is likely to throw up, and put that one near an open window. We drove round the suburbs of Maidenhead, coaxing the addresses from confused teenagers and delivering them. I made a point of ringing each doorbell, on the pretext of making sure they got home OK, but also to make sure that the other parents shared my disturbed night. We got home and Son No. 2 crawled into bed. I checked the floor of the car and found the usual debris from a teenage party. A bottle of Vodka; a poker score-card and a blue video. In the back of the estate was a pile of dirty clothes. This turned out to be Joshua. I knew it was Joshua but Joshua didn't know it was Joshua. I carried him to a spare bed, made sure he was on his side and went back to sleep.

At midday, Son No. 2 emerged. "I left my Walkman at the party. Will you drive me round?"

"Ask your mother."

I Believe

November 1986

It was raining hard and I was walking briskly the quarter of a mile from Acton Town tube station to the nearby Conservative Club. As from nowhere, someone stepped out from behind the shadows and accosted me. I felt for my wallet.

"Excuse me" he said "Do you believe in God?"

I was not ready for a theological exchange. "Yes" I replied, walking briskly on. He moved on to his next question, keeping pace with me. "When did you last go to Church?" That was easy. "Yesterday, twice." (I had just attended two Remembrance Day services.)

He was neither impressed nor deterred by my zeal. "Have you read the New Testament?" Dim memories of Scripture "O" Level swam before my eyes – and the Conservative Club was not yet in sight.

"Yes" I said, asking myself how many other God-fearing, Church-attending, Scripture-reading people he had accosted in South Acton that evening. No one had got round the course as far as I had, so there was a pause before he asked the next of his questions. "Do you believe everything in it?" This was tricky.

"Ah" I replied" Do you mean, do I believe that it is a factual record of what happened; or are you asking if I accept all the moral imperatives of the Gospel?"

He ducked the question and moved on "Have you broken any of Our Lord's commandments?"

That was easy. "Yes"

He then got to the final question "Will you come and repent of your sins with me next Sunday?"

"No"

He stopped and looked at me in horror. Then he looked down at his book for the verdict. "You are an unrepentant sinner" he said "Your soul will be damned and consumed by flames in Hell."

And, as if to prove his point, I crossed the threshold of the Acton Conservative Club.

The Burglary

November 1986

My interest in crime prevention has been re-awakened because we have been burgled. I don't complain too much as it was only the second time in 25 years. Statistically, it was long overdue. Others must have had had their pictures removed while the Young collection remained intact.

We were burgled because the expensive burglar alarm we bought three years ago failed to go off.

The burglar alarm is a three year old Alsatian, the guarantee on which has expired. (I describe him as an Alsatian, but he tells me that he and his colleagues have consulted an advertising agency and have been told they have an image problem. They are being rebranded as German Shepherd Dogs.)

As with many politicians, beneath the dog's gruff exterior there beats a warm heart. So warm in fact that he was glad to have some company in the small hours of the morning; particularly as the company brought him some fillet steak of a quality way beyond the budget of his hosts. While he was consuming this, his benefactors were helping themselves to the family silver.

In the morning, when we discovered the worst, he was rebuked. He was told his conditions of service were under review; that his attitude towards strangers had become a liability; and that we expected a sharp improvement in his performance. On the football pitch, it would have been the yellow card.

He looked contrite.

Two hours later, a CID officer arrived to solve the crime. The dog bit him, unhesitatingly, in the ankle.

A Bad Week

January 1987

It had been a bad week in the House of Commons. I recalled the story of a colleague who came home from a late night sitting at breakfast time, for the third consecutive day. His wife had left him this welcoming note.

"The day before yesterday, you came home yesterday. Yesterday, you came home today. If, today, you come home tomorrow, you will find that I left yesterday."

I was not in the same sort of trouble after a sequence of late nights, but by the Friday when I got home, I was irritable.

Son No. 2 was behaving badly and eventually I picked him up and shouted at him. "Stop it. You're ten now, why can't you behave like a ten year old?"

"Put him down" said my wife "He's only seven."

***

The Misprint

February 1987

Any columnist can expect to find his work enlivened by the occasional misprint. "Not" instead of "now" can dramatically interfere with the logical development of an argument.

But thanks to technology and the introduction of standard paragraphs, the number of intermediaries one can blame for such errors is being fast reduced.

Misprints are not always easy to spot. If one is signing Ministerial correspondence late at night, a few might go unnoticed. As a Minister at the DHSS, I got a letter from an MP who complained that one of his constituents had not been sent her milk and butter tokens.

An enterprising secretary in the typing pool had typed up a letter for my signature beginning, "I was sorry to hear your constituent's mild and bitter tokens had gone astray."

But she was outbid by another secretary who typed up a letter in response to a Labour MP, complaining about the threatened closure of a cottage hospital in his constituency.

The gist of the reply was that, with efficient administration and modern drugs, the productivity of a hospital could be increased. People did not have to spend so much time recuperating, so fewer beds were needed for a given number of what the NHS is pleased to call "in-patient episodes."

The climax of my letter was meant to end with the declaration. "The whole thrust of this administration's policy, in contrast to that of our predecessor's, is to promote bed management."

But the "e" in bed had been replaced by an "a", significantly changing the message. Mercifully, my eyes had not closed as they sped over this letter at the bottom of the third red box. It was returned for correction, with a message saying that I hoped that the manager of the typing pool wouldn't give her a bedtime.

***

The Channel Tunnel

March 1987

Bad news for the country's cyclists; the campaign to get their bicycles on British Rail's Channel Tunnel trains has been derailed.

Their Lordships were petitioned by the Friends of the Earth and asked to amend the Channel Tunnel Bill, for friendly and earthy reasons, to permit the carriage of bicycles. British Rail objected, claiming there was no market.

I had pointed out, when the Bill was in the Commons, that the airlines carried bicycles across the channel free - doubtless at more inconvenience to themselves than to anyone running a rail service –

so they clearly thought there was a market. But British Rail were not impressed; and their Lordships, perhaps with their best cycling days behind them, did not press the point. (With wheelchairs, the outcome would have been different.)

The British Rail argument that there is "no market for bicycles on trains" was punctured some time ago. When I tried to get bicycles on commuter trains, British Rail told me there was no demand. I persevered, and they were allowed on for a trial period. The experiment had to be stopped – too many people wanted to put their bicycles on the trains and British Rail could not cope. And commuters complained about oil from bicycle chains on their suits.

British Rail then relented; they would encourage the cycling fraternity to use the train, and indeed asked me to feature in a suitable poster. Stations all over the country featured the member for Ealing Acton plus children plus bicycles. (This campaign coincided with a General Election when the local Labour Party – ingeniously, but unsuccessfully – tried to score the cost of the posters against my election expenses.)

Peace with British Rail ended when they re-used the poster – without my consent – to advertise a new policy which involved unwelcome changes for cyclists.

Now, to get their own back, British Rail are likely to commission rolling stock for the Channel Tunnel trains which will carry cars, horses, every conceivable form of luggage and freight - except the bicycle. If you want to take your bicycle across the channel by train, you will have to catch an ordinary train to Dover; bicycle to the Eurotunnel Terminal at Cheriton; and then put it on the shuttle run by private enterprise.

***

Back to Oxford

March 1987

It is not often that I return to Oxford, where I first cut my political teeth in the 1960s. I remember sitting in my room, grappling with symbolic logic in preparation for some exams, success in which was a precondition for remaining there for the next two years. There was a knock on the door, and a glamorous blonde shimmered in. "I am a Young Conservative" she said "Are you interested?"

I was and joined the Oxford University Conservative Association. Thus began a life-long interest in the British Constitution, Parliamentary Democracy and the Conservative Party. Harold Macmillan, Rab Butler, Edward Boyle, Iain Macleod all came to address OUCA and influenced my impressionable young mind.

On one occasion, OUCA invited a Cabinet Minister to Oxford, offering him dinner beforehand, in a five star hotel. This was in the days of relaxed security, and before the creation of the Government Car Service. The Minister said he would come by train, and asked to be met at the station. As was usual in University politics – and has sometimes happened to the Party nationally - there were within the Conservatives two warring factions.

Group B, who had missed out on election to the key offices and were excluded from the dinner, devised an alternative strategy. They sent a telegram (older readers can explain to younger readers what a telegram was) to the controlling Group A, saying that the Minister could not come in time for dinner and would make his own way to the venue for the speech.

The Minister was then met at the station by Group B, and he was of course unable to distinguish between one set of Conservative students and another. He was regally entertained and delivered in time for his speech, suitably refreshed, to Group A, who were mystified as to how their guest had fallen into enemy hands.

Now, without comparing myself to those giants of the 1960s, twenty five years later history had turned full circle. I found myself addressing OUCA on current political issues.

One face in the audience seemed familiar; it was Son No. 1 who had turned up – out of loyalty I suspect, rather than in the hope of learning something new. Or perhaps he was hoping to discuss with me later the vexed question of student grants and parental contributions.

That visit to Oxford went better than my last one. Going through some old books at home in the late 1960s, I came across a first edition of Piers Plowman – one of the first books ever to be printed. It had been given to my family in the 18th century in lieu of the payment of a debt. It was of some value, and wasted in the library at home. I contacted the Librarian at Christ Church, and offered it on permanent loan. I said I would bring it round on my next visit to the dreaming spires, in a few days time.

He replied, accepting my offer, as follows.

"Dear Young,

Many thanks for your offer of the first edition of Piers Plowman on permanent loan; this will be a significant attraction to our Library. It is kind of you to offer to bring it with you next week.

Could you, at the same time, please return AJ Ayer's "Language Truth and Logic", which you borrowed in 1960 and is still outstanding."

***

A Statutory Instrument

April 1987

I had not realised quite how interventionist government had become – and a Conservative Government at that – until I was appointed a member of the Third Standing Committee to debate a Statutory Instrument on the Draft Revised Code of Recommendations for the Welfare of Domestic Fowls, Ducks, Rabbits and Turkeys. Being a conscientious man, I got the relevant documents from the Vote Office and read them in bed the night before.

It was then that I discovered, in paragraph 48 of the Code on Rabbits, that we had a policy on the length of a rabbit's toenail. Admittedly, it had been omitted from the manifesto to make way for more pressing social and economic issues, but there it was in black and white. The little fellows need them cut at regular intervals. I turned to the Code on Ducks to see where we stood on duck's toenails. But we don't, and neither do ducks as their feet are webbed.

But we do have a policy on turkey toenails, and the younger reader should read no further. "To avoid injury to hens during mating, even when saddled, the last joint of the inside toes of male breeding birds should be removed." I suppose it is a small price for a turkey to pay for the privilege of pleasuring his bride, but I was relieved that the process of evolution had removed this design fault from homo sapiens and the concomitant need for surgery.

I had not planned to speak in the debate, but was moved to do so. The first two speeches were from the two Front Bench spokesmen – one an ex-butcher, the other a prosperous land-owning farmer. (The farmer was the Labour MP, the butcher the Tory.) The debate was not adversarial, perhaps because the Tory made a living slaughtering the animals reared by his opponent. When they had finished, I rose to my feet and asked why an MP elected on a non-interventionist, deregulatory ticket should support this instrument of micro-management. The Government Whip on the Committee looked up from his correspondence and stared at me until I sat down. The Minister then put me back in my box with a withering reply about the political imperatives of animal welfare.

I got home that night and Daughter No. 2 asked me what I had done at school that day. I told her. "Due to my attendance at the House, rabbits will now have shorter toenails, and turkeys can mate in comfort." And young people are turning away from politics.

***

A Novice in the Whips Office

July 1987

Shortly after being elected in 1974, I joined the Whips Office. Their job is to make sure that the colleagues appear in the right lobby at the right time, and say the right things, at least in public. To give more detail would be to break the Whips' vow of Omerta. Silence, in the world of the Mafia. To discharge their duties, the Whips need to know where their flock live and where they are likely to be found. (Not always the same locations). And thus one needs their telephone numbers.

The Whips are also used by the party leader for man-management; Margaret Thatcher has always been a good entertainer of the troops and, shortly after her election as Leader and my appointment to the Whips Office, she wanted an up-to-date list of the names of the wives of the colleagues, so they could be invited to a party along with their husbands.

And thus it was that a fresh-faced unknown new boy in the Whips Office approached the senior statesmen and Knights of the Shires in his party, notebook in hand, with two questions.

"What is your home telephone number; and what is your wife's Christian name?"

Some misunderstood my motives.

***

From Russia with Love

November 1987

The invitation from Ealing College to show 30 visiting teachers from the Soviet Union round the House of Commons was accepted with alacrity.

Here was an opportunity, I reasoned, not just to challenge the prejudices of those with a distorted appreciation of our parliamentary democracy; but, through them, to reach out to the impressionable young minds whom they taught. Further, I could show them a confident and alert right-of-centre administration, successfully steering a market-led economy along the path of material prosperity and contrast it with the austerity of the Soviet regime.

We met in the Central Lobby. I spoke slowly, using monosyllables where possible, and explained that we had two Chambers in our Parliament. One of the hosts sidled up to me. "They are all fluent in English, and have the equivalent of a First Class honours degree in British Constitution. I suggest you raise your game."

"Right" I said "Let us see the Chamber in action." I steered them past a mass lobby for the Campaign for Nuclear Disarmament. "Is that gentleman all right?" asked a Russian, as a middle-aged man disappeared under a sea of beards and placards.

"He should be" I replied "He is the Secretary of State for Defence."

We went up to the Strangers' Gallery. The House had been sitting continuously for 26 hours, and eight unshaven, somnolent men were in the Chamber, in relaxed postures, surrounded by the parliamentary debris of Order Papers and discarded speeches.

"Where are the other 630?" I was asked. "Working in their constituencies" I replied.

"Why is that Conservative MP wearing a skirt?" "He's a Scot – that is a kilt"

"How does the MP who has been suspended from the Chamber represent his constituents?" "Why are you abolishing the Greater London Council?" "Why is it important for the Speaker to wear an 18th century wig?"

"I know you will all want to see the House of Lords" I replied.

We repaired to the Upper House.

"Why are they all sitting there with their eyes closed?" "They are listening to the amplifiers set into the back of their seats. And concentrating on the debate."

"The man with the moustache and no chin who is speaking, how did he become a Lord?" "His great-grandfather's great-grandmother slept with the King."

"Why does that bench have armrests?" "That's for the bishops; they used to get so drunk that they fell off."

Sixty uncomprehending eyes stared up at me. "Look, I've done all the talking" I said. "Let's have a drink on the Terrace and you tell me how you run things back home."

Private Member's Bill

March 1988

Getting a new Bill onto the Statute Book can be tough. Ask the Ministers piloting the Poll Tax (sorry, Community Charge) Bill through the House.

But it need not be so. It took me two and a half minutes to get my Bill through all its stages in the House of Commons.

The Land Registry Bill (Lords) completed its passage through the Upper House on a Tuesday evening. It was a Private Members Bill which opened the Land Registry for public inspection and it was a social reform that I supported. After the Lords had sanctioned it, it was then entrusted to a messenger to take it to the Lower House, tied up with some red ribbon. He was clearly a slow mover, as the Bill did not arrive in our place until late on Wednesday afternoon.

The moment it arrived, I put it on the Order Paper for that Friday, at 2.30pm. This is a time when those MPs who are in on a Friday are in the car park, getting ready to drive home, as formal business concludes at 2.30pm.

Then came the tricky bit. Any objection after 2.30 blocks a Bill and it goes to the back of the legislative queue – the equivalent of landing on a snake in Snakes and Ladders. The Clerk read the title of the Bill. No one objected, so the Bill moved one square along the board. There was then a duet between myself and the Deputy Speaker. The opening line was hers "Second Reading what day?"

"Now Sir" I replied, although the Deputy Speaker was a lady.

"The question is that the Bill be read a Second time." She declaimed in a bold soprano. What happened to the First reading remained a mystery, but I looked down at my score and sang "Aye."

"Committee Stage what day?" she crooned.

"Now Sir"

It was time for an interval so we could clear our throats. The Serjeant-at-Arms marched up the Chamber, removed the Mace from the table, and hung it on the hooks below. He retreated and we resumed the performance.

"The question is that Clause 1 stand part of the Bill."

"Aye". By now, a small crowd had formed at the Bar of the House, and they joined in the chorus. As each clause was invited to stand part of the Bill, the Ayes got louder, in a harmonious C sharp.

There was a second interval, the Mace was restored to the table and I was asked whether I had the Queen's approval. This could have been a show stopper. A Privy Councillor is required for this role. I had found one in the Member's Dining Room having a late lunch and had summoned him to the Chamber. He rose to his feet, bowed to signify Her Majesty's benediction on my Bill and went back for his pudding.

"The question is that the Bill be read a Third time" sang the heroine.

"Aye" we baritones shouted in a final crescendo as the curtain fell and a fresh piece of social legislation thudded on to the statute book.

***

Don't rely on the Irish

May 1988

The Bill to phase paybeds out of NHS hospitals was going through Parliament in the 1970s, when the Labour Government no longer had an overall majority. The Standing Committee considering the Bill line by line had an equal number of Labour and Conservative MPs, with the balance of power being held by an Ulster Unionist.

I do him no discourtesy by describing him as an infrequent attender at our Committee. However, for complicated Irish reasons, he told me he did not want to be seen to be sustaining the Labour Party in office. He assured me, as the Opposition Whip on the Bill, that he would vote with us whenever he was needed. However, whereas most MPs need six minutes to get to the Division Lobby, he would need six hours notice so he could catch a plane and fly over.

One day, it was clear we would be voting on some key amendments. I got on the telephone to Belfast and summoned my new friend. "To be sure George, I'll be right over".

With some difficulty, we kept the debate going while British Airways and London Transport did their stuff. A breathless Irishman burst into the committee room. The faces of the Labour MPs dropped when they saw him arrive. The Conservatives were delighted, as his arrival meant they could stop developing their arguments, which were beginning to become repetitive and thereby testing the patience of the Committee Chairman.

The debate ended; the vote was called. It was a tie, until the Irishman voted. And then he voted. With the Labour Party.

***

The Barbour

November 1988

For the last ten years, my vulnerable frame has been protected from the English winter by a blue anorak. I have never claimed that it was elegant. Indeed, one of its merits was that no right-minded person would help himself to it at the end of a party, if there was another coat available. It kept me warm on my bicycle.

But like so much of my wardrobe to which I had become attached, my wife decided that it must go. Its fate was sealed when she saw it being interviewed on College Green on News at Ten, when it contrasted badly with the expensive number sported by my Labour opposite number. She felt that Ealing Acton's parliamentary representative should advertise the prosperity he kept on talking about, so she went and bought a smart new one. (Coat, not representative). The old anorak is hanging in a charity shop, waiting for a thin gentleman who is six foot four, of modest means and with an uncritical wife to acquire it.

Its successor came with a jar of Vaseline and a book complimenting me on my choice. Its first outing was to Twickenham, to watch England play the tourists at rugby. Arriving late, I put it on the pile in the hospitality suite and went in to the lunch to listen to a former England International supplement his income by telling bad jokes and incorrectly forecasting the result.

After the game, we adjourned to the hospitality suite to celebrate England's success. I had to leave before the serious singing began. I stared at the pile, with hundreds of identical coats on it. My wife clearly knew what she was doing, as this is what One Wore at Rugger Internationals. I never had this problem with the blue anorak. Fortunately, I had left my radiopager in the pocket. So straight to a telephone to dial the number that activated the bleep. Then a sprint to the celebration party to ask for silence. And then back to the coats. A bleep was heard. Like a St Bernard looking for a skier buried in an avalanche, I dived into the coats, found mine and headed off for the constituency wine and cheese.

***

Libelled!

May 1989

I can reveal exclusively in this column that I have now joined the ranks of those politicians who have been libelled. My attention was drawn, as they say, to a radical publication on Higher Education in which I was confused with someone with a similar name, and attributed with views which I do not hold and associates with whom I do not consort.

I reached for the telephone to instruct my solicitor to do something more exciting than buy and sell flats in Ealing, or redraft my will to reflect the arrival of fresh offspring.

I told him of the injury to my reputation. "Open and shut case" he replied. "They have no defence." I reflected on the opportunities for investing the ample funds that would be needed to repair the injury to my reputation. I was not expecting seven figures, but five would not be out of place.

Perhaps my ten year old car had seen better days. The holes in the tennis court gave the home team a welcome advantage, but the time might have come to have it resurfaced. The dinner jacket was doubtless smart when it was commissioned in the 1970's, but the lads at the Carnarvon Hotel in Ealing were wearing something trendier at the Acton Conservative Club Ladies Night. And it was beginning to pinch around the waist.

Negotiations proceeded satisfactorily. Large numbers of books were pulped; smaller numbers were recalled from bookshops; abject letters of apology were drafted and exchanged. My injury was dressed and my reputation nursed back to health.

I finally got round to asking my solicitor the question that really mattered. How much?

"Sorry about this, old boy; bad news. Not a bean. The author is out of work and the publisher is a man of straw. Now we've made them pulp the book, they have no income either." And then the killer blow. "I'll send you my bill when I've worked out how much time this has taken me."

***

Silver Wedding

July 1989

This column is not in the ego-massaging business. When a politician uses space in his column to heap praise on himself, it means a General Election is imminent or he is threatened with de-selection. Neither condition is currently fulfilled but, that said, there is cause for modest celebration. My wife and I celebrate this week our Silver Wedding anniversary.

Twenty five years ago, in Christ Church Cathedral, the conjugal knot was tied by the Bishop of Oxford. He clearly did a thorough job, as securely tied it has subsequently remained. Sir Alec Douglas-Home was Prime Minister; the Parliamentary Secretary at the Ministry of Pensions and National Insurance was an obscure lady called Margaret Thatcher. The Health Minister was Enoch Powell.

Income tax was seven shillings and sixpence in the pound. I was earning £750 a year in the City, and driving an Austin Healey 3000. I had lots of hair and no spectacles, a condition now reversed. It was pre-Beatles, and England had a decent football team.

We knew little then about Ealing. It produced comedians rather than politicians. We would pass through Ealing Broadway station to and from Paddington at speed in a brown GWR railway carriage, drawn by a steam engine.

Little did we know it at the time, but as we plighted our troths, two bodies in Ealing were also being conjoined – Acton and Ealing Councils. Unlike ours, it was an arranged marriage in which romance and courtship played no part. Although they had lived next door for ages, Acton and Ealing had never really liked each other. Indeed, there had been some bitter exchanges over the garden fence. Class difference was whispered to be the problem, as W5 looked down on W3. But neither could survive on their own, it had been decreed by the Redcliff-Maude Commission on local government, so they must unite. Ealing Acton was a constituency of beauty and contrast it was said; all the beauty being in Ealing and all the contrast in Acton.

As we celebrate our 25 years, there is no corresponding euphoria at Ealing Town Hall. Indeed, there is talk of separation. Acton regards itself as the betrayed bride, having given up her name and her dowry of a town hall to sustain prosperous Ealing in the style to which it is accustomed. It has lost its own cinema, local newspaper and Member of Parliament.

And yet, in 25 years time, it may be that the London Borough of Ealing is still there. Whether we are still part of it is in the hands of the Almighty – and the electorate. (Or, as it later turned out, the Boundary Commission)

The Wasps

August 1989

This week's column is not for the faint-hearted. It has a "PG" label affixed to it. You have been warned.

Our enjoyment of the fine summer weather has been marred by the presence of wasps. If we eat out, they join us in the garden. If we eat in, they gatecrash the party through the kitchen door. If we close the kitchen door, the Aga makes the temperature inside intolerable.

So the family have been put on a seek-and-destroy mission for the wasps' nest. The seeking to be done by the method I learned on my grandfather's knee. You sprinkle flour on the wings of the wasp.

Three consequences follow. First, the beast heads for the nearest Accident and Emergency unit, based at the local nest, to get the flour removed. Second, it does so at a modest pace because of its handicap. Third, its progress is clearly visible, as the finest and whitest flour has been used.

After seek, destroy. Once the nest is located, you wait until they are all inside and tucked up in bed. Block the entrance with a rag soaked in petrol; light the touch paper and retire. My grandfather was not a sentimental man. So much for the theory.

Attracting the wasps was no problem. A jar on a garden bench half-filled with water, with honey smeared on the inside, produced some early punters. My wife, well-clad, stood over the jar, a bag of unbleached plain flour in one hand and, for maximum coverage, a sieve in the other. The family stood around, prepared to follow the trail.

The first wasp was overdone. Instead of one part flour to three parts wasp, my wife reversed the ingredients. Laden with flour, the wasp plummeted to the ground and started the long walk home. The next wasp was hit on one wing, and could only fly in circles. The third one was treated as my grandfather would have wished, but then headed for the top of the tallest tree in the garden.

We never found the nest and gave up after half an hour. But fortified by eating all the high protein flour in the garden later that day, the wasps have never looked healthier.

***

The Passport

September 1989

Our American holiday for three was nearly a holiday for two. My wife's passport had been despatched to the US Embassy for the insertion of a visa, allowing ample time for processing. She had been to the US once before, 25 years earlier, and had left neither owing taxes, selling drugs nor preaching Marxism. There should have been no trouble. Indeed, she was proposing to inject useful purchasing power into the US economy via the Walt Disney Corporation.

Five days before departure, the passport had still not been returned. A lady at the US Embassy, speaking with a perfect Oxford accent, told me that the passport could be reclaimed in person. So I queued for 90 minutes along with others, all with a common ambition to fly to America.

When I reached the front of the queue, I asked for the passport back. My wife's date of birth was fed into the computer. There was bad news. "If we return the passport now, Sir Young, we stamp it "Visa Refused." Your wife may be denied admission."

My wife does not enjoy crossing the Atlantic by air; crossing it twice in one day after being denied entry would test her patience beyond endurance – though the blow would have been softened by not having to accompany Daughter No. 2 on the rides at Disneyworld. The computer then spat out a docket. "But the good news is that we posted it back yesterday with the visa." The value of this good news depreciated with the passage of four days and no passport. Mr

Forrest of Royal Mail was contacted and he flushed the conduits of the postal system between Grosvenor Square and our postman's round. No passport was found. "They sometimes get stolen" we were told.

It is possible to get a replacement passport within three hours. The ordeal is similar to that confronting Pamino and Pamina in Mozart's Magic Flute, but we completed the course to the satisfaction of the judges at 5.30 on the eve of take-off. We were woken the next morning by the cheerful whistle of our postman. On the mat was the original passport. Its envelope has been sent to Mr Forrest to conduct a post-mortem. My friend at the Southall Marriage Bureau tells me that the second passport is worth much more than the £15 we paid for it. But no, we have sent it back to the Home Office.

***

Student Grants

December 1989

Christmas being a time for the family, I drove down to Exeter to retrieve Son No. 2 from University there. Entering his room, I looked hard for evidence of intellectual activity. CDs, yes; packs of cards, yes; pin-ups, definitely; beer cans, everywhere. Of essays or books relating to history or sociology – the young man's chosen subjects – not a trace. On the table there was a letter from his bank manager, using terms that I instantly recognised. When he turned up, I asked him why income and expenditure were not in balance. There was a passing reference to the size of his allowance compared with that allotted to his contemporaries, and a plausible story about the initial capital expenditure involved in being a serious student – books, membership of various societies, fees paid in advance. Under cross-examination, he denied any extravagance in lifestyle.

He did indeed look hungry, so I offered to buy him lunch at an Indian restaurant of his choice. Before we went in, I glanced at the menu pinned in the window. The Lamb Passanda was selling at a comfortable premium over that in the Ealing Tandoori. Clearly, this was a haunt for the well-heeled gourmet.

The Head Waiter greeted Son No. 2 with the deference extended to MPs by the policemen at the Members' Entrance. "Good afternoon Mr Young, your usual table?" We were guided to a secluded corner. "Pint of lager and four poppadums? I see your young lady is not with you today, Mr Young."

In a fragrant waft of Indian spices, Son No. 2's financial alibi and protestations of thrift drifted into the streets of Exeter, filled with Christmas shoppers.

***

Leading the Blind

January 1990

No one is keener than I am to help the blind and partially sighted, though those who witnessed a recent incident may doubt that claim.

I was eating an apple as I approached a pair of swing doors in the Mall in Ealing. Each half of the door was about two foot wide, so I could easily get through by pushing just one half open. I went through, then glanced over my shoulder to see if I could hold it open for anyone behind. Hoving into view was a man with impaired vision, preceded by his dog. So I stood at my post, door in hand, as the pair approached.

It then became obvious that this was not only not going to be polite; it was going to be very dangerous. The dog was heading for the open half of the pair of swing doors, which he would get through; but his master was heading at speed for the closed half.

Clearly, that half of the door had to be opened promptly. I liberated my second hand by putting the apple in my mouth and pushed open the other half – keeping open the first half for the dog. But I was then rooted right in the middle of the oncoming procession. Time was running out; there was no one else around to hold a door. A shouted warning was impossible because of the apple. Removing the apple meant abandoning a door and either felling the dog or its master.

Readers may have worked out a solution to this social dilemma, but I ran out of time.

The three of us picked ourselves up from an untidy heap on the floor. I brushed the dog hairs off my suit and retrieved my apple from the dog's mouth. I apologised profusely and mercifully no harm was done.

I explained my predicament and asked what I should have done. I should have left both doors closed was the answer. The dog would then have stopped.

***

Down with Flu

February 1990

Older readers may recall a film entitled The Cockleshell Heroes, a war film whose heroes used phrases now extinct – "Jerry's kite hit the drink" – "Bandits at three o'clock". These men displayed superhuman courage. Younger readers need to know that the stiff upper lips in the film were attached to Trevor Howard, José Ferrar and Victor Maddern. Based on a true story during World War Two, our heroes travelled by train, then by canoe to Bordeaux, to attach limpet mines to ships of the German Navy. I cannot remember exactly what happened to them, as I saw the film in 1955. But I recall the ingenuity with which they evaded the protection surrounding the enemy fleet. I think something messy happened to Victor Maddern, which meant he had gone long before the National Anthem was played at the end of the performance.

Lying in bed recently, the victim of a virus, the analogy seemed appropriate and I knew how the German admiral must have felt.

My body's defences are pretty good, with a robust immune system. Potential invaders are identified at an early stage and eliminated. My white cells are feared throughout bacteriological circles. Years of cycling, playing squash and eating Indian food have paid off and built good resistance to all bugs. Perhaps a touch of complacency had crept into those on patrol.

A few days ago, a virus paddling a cockleshell loaded with explosives slipped into my bloodstream. The mines floating around didn't blow it up; it didn't show up on the radar screen of my central nervous system and the sentries must have been asleep. Perhaps the virus had blackened its face.

But it got through in the dead of night, keeping up its courage by whistling the tune from the Dambusters, and shining its waterproof torch on the map of my tributaries and arteries paddling relentlessly towards its target. It broke through all defences and attached some limpet mines below the water line near the engine room and paddled off. After a massive eruption, the body politic was laid low. It sank gently into the bed, rocking in the current. Fires broke out everywhere and the temperature became unbearable.

An alarm was sounded. Sister ships from the Young family were ordered to evacuate less they fall victims as well. The Headquarters of Counter Intelligence – the health centre – was contacted in the morning. "Yes indeed," they told me. Enemy agents had got behind the lines; whole settlements had been laid low by the virus. It would take days to repair the damage. But our allies, the Americans, were flying over some vaccines.

Out of Date

March 1990

My wife is an infrequent visitor to the House of Commons. The
twenty miles from home to the constituency in West London is
within her usual radius, but the next seven miles to Westminster is
not. Making a rare visit to the House last week, she presented herself
at the St Stephen's Entrance. Her pass was promptly confiscated by a
vigilant policeman. It was five years out of date.

I rebuked her gently for this oversight, pointing out that the expiry
date was in capital letters on the pass.

She joined me at a time when morale was low. A well-briefed
constituent had just been to lobby me about the Government's
Employment Training Scheme. As we sat down over a cup of tea in
the Pugin Room, he took out his notebook. "I don't think you're
going to need that" I told him "There's not much I can tell you that
you don't know already."

"I am aware of that" he replied "It's for making notes of what I tell
you."

My wife without her pass and me without my ego were a sad couple,
so we resolved to go out to dinner. We ate agreeably at a restaurant
we had first patronised in the sixties, but this time counting the
calories instead of the cost.

As the coffee was served, I asked for the bill "Add on ten percent" I
said generously, handing the waiter my flexible friend.

Moments later he was back. "I am sorry, sir. Your card has expired."

The Last Match

April 1990

The House of Commons has numerous All Party Groups, one of which has been in my control for the past 16 years. The All Party Squash Team, which I captain.

Organising fixtures is difficult, because we like to play during the day, whereas most teams like to play in the evenings. We like to play in the day because, if we play in the evenings, we have to run in our squash kit from the courts in Millbank to the division lobbies in the House of Commons in six minutes, whenever the division bell goes. This depletes our stock of calories which we need to win the match. So we end up playing people who work shifts and can play in the daytime – policemen, firemen, doctors – all of whom are frighteningly fit.

Getting MPs in to the right division lobby at the right time requires the attention of 20 Whips. Getting five MPs onto the squash court requires equivalent coercion and cajoling. Otherwise they don't turn up.

Two days before what turned out to be our last fixture, five of us were pledged to play against a local firm, who are by Appointment Purveyors of Groceries to Her Majesty. Then, in the words of St Luke, Chapter 14 verse 18, my team all with one consent began to make excuses.

The first said unto me he hath been appointed unto a Statutory Instrument Committee and the Whip would be sorely displeased if he were not in attendance. I pray thee have me excused.

And another said that an ailment of the fibula had rendered him indisposed and his apothecary could not be held accountable if he disported himself on court in violent exercise. And so on until there were only two of us left.

The biblical option of going quickly into the streets and lanes of Westminster and bringing in hither the poor, and the maimed, and the halt, and the blind would not have delivered me a team to beat the grocers.

With reluctance, I rang up the Captain of the opposing team and explained. We agreed that the two of us should, nonetheless, have a private contest.

I contacted the only member of the team who had not produced an excuse and told his secretary the match was cancelled.

SIR GEORGE YOUNG
AGE 47
HEIGHT: 6ft 4½in WEIGHT: 13st CHEST: 42in
WAIST: 35in HIPS: 42½in AROUND THIGH: 23½in
NECK: 15in SHOE SIZE: 10½

Halfway through our match, there was a knock on the door of the court. The member without the excuse for not playing had turned up to play, the message from his secretary not having been received. His arrival was opportune. We were two games all, but, moving from St Luke to St Matthew, Chapter 25, my opponent still had some oil in his lamp, whereas I had been more foolish.

I transferred the score to my Parliamentary colleague and moved to the gallery to give him moral encouragement, believing his vessels to be full of oil. He lost.

I offered him my resignation and he accepted it. The team, I fear, is no more.

The Earpiece

May 1990

The picture on your television is familiar. In the background, Big Ben. In the foreground, two windswept MPs of opposing views. In the middle ground, some stationary traffic, some tourists looking for Westminster Abbey and some pigeons. Some fresh malady has struck the Government and two colleagues – hand-picked for their ready availability – are being asked for a diagnosis.

Occasionally I appear in this role. A microphone is affixed to the inside of my shirt by a sound engineer with cold hands. I am then invited to recall what I had for breakfast while the sound engineer recalibrates the instrument for the right decibel count. I am then told I am one foot taller than the last person they interviewed and so a new tripod is required, with a box for the cameraman to stand on. I am asked to move six inches to my right, to wait for the bus to pass – and then off we go. The nation is reassured that, contrary to any conflicting evidence, everything is for the best in the best of all possible worlds.

Thus it was that, a few days ago, I found myself with a parliamentary colleague beside me, a pigeon behind me and two cameras in front of me. I had had the cold hands treatment and we were on air in one minute. Another technological prop was then introduced – the earpiece.

If you see a politician being interviewed and swatting a mosquito on his right ear, he is in fact adjusting his earpiece, which enables him to hear the questioner in a remote studio.

My earpiece was in place and the engineer was about to affix one to my colleague. She then announced that she refused to wear earpieces in public – (though she had giggled when the sound engineer fitted a microphone near her cleavage). At which point the producer shouted "On Air"

A question from an interrogator in Shepherds Bush arrived in my right ear. I looked squarely at the wrong camera and answered it.

Another question arrived from Shepherds Bush of which I only heard half. It was interrupted by the sound engineer saying "We got a mad woman 'ere what won't wear an earpiece." I answered what I thought the question might have been.

It then got tricky. The remote interrogator announced he had a question for my colleague, which he put. My colleague, not being plugged into the network, continued to smile alternately at each camera. I had heard her question, and offered to repeat it to her and, as a bonus, to tell her the answer.

Too late. The interviewer announced to a confused world that there were technical problems at Westminster and we were cut off.

I ran off to my next appointment, followed by two panting technicians. One wanted his microphone back. And the other wanted the earpiece.

***

Pray Silence for...

June 1990

As in other callings, so in after dinner speaking; there are amateurs and professionals. The former do it because they like to and receive no payment. The latter do so because they have to and receive payment – often in readies from the Social Secretary after the meal.

I am in the former category, perhaps because the market has so far failed to put a value on my performance. But I frequently speak at functions where the other speakers are paid; and handsomely paid, at that.

If one speaks regularly on the Ealing Acton circuit, one cannot deliver the same speech time after time, though some anecdotes may occasionally recur. (My discerning electorate would soon vote for a new purveyor of after dinner jokes.) But if one is on the national circuit, alighting but once in Ealing Acton, one can survive with one "core" speech, with regional variations, committed effortlessly to memory and delivered with apparent spontaneity.

So readers will understand the feeling of injustice as I struggle to produce something fresh for each occasion and deliver it for free; and this professional rides into town, recites his set speech and gallops off with £800 in his pocket.

Thus it was that I was addressing a local organisation, warming them up for the professional. He listened with ill-disguised contempt for my performance, though he carefully noted down the better jokes to freshen up his repertoire.

The Toastmaster then introduced him as the Speaker We had All Come to Hear, begging the question of the status of the Speaker Who Had Just Sat Down. The former stood up. But he had misjudged his audience. Ladies were present – and what is more, ladies from Ealing rather than Acton. He started off with a joke about the man with an iron bar and weak wrists. It fell flat; but once he was on the tram-lines, he had nowhere else to go. Even if the men thought him funny, they dared not laugh because the wife was next to them, unamused.

He got the bird, and I can't say I was sorry. It was as if a non-League side had beaten Manchester United. But worse was to come.

After the dinner was over, there was an altercation in the gentleman's cloakroom. The Chairman of the Social Committee, in a heated conversation with the Speaker We Had All Come to Hear, was asserting that the services acquired from him by the society were not of the appropriate quality. He had had to apologise to many of the ladies, whose sensitivities had been offended. Even he had not understood the joke about the bar of soap in the bath. Therefore the agreed quantity of notes, recently acquired from the tombola, would not be handed over. The case for the defence was that, as the professional only had one speech, there could never have been any doubt about what was being acquired.

I left. Perhaps, after all, there is something to be said for being an amateur.

Top of the Pops

July 1990

It is some 30 years since I went to a Pop Concert. A colleague at work had acquired, through the informal market, a block of tickets for the Beatles. Anxious to win the heart of my wife-to-be, who was one of their fans, I purchased two tickets at an informal price and invited her along. I forget the venue and indeed the songs they sang. But I recall the seats were covered with cellophane, such was the hysteria expected from my contemporaries.

Dim memories of the occasion were recalled when Daughter No. 2 announced over breakfast "I've got four tickets for New Kids on the Block." "I know" I said "You bought them with my Visa card."

She wanted me to take her to the Docklands Arena and I agreed. I agreed, that is, to take her there; but not to go in. This would enable her, I pointed out, to have safe conduct to and from Docklands, without the inhibiting presence of her father at the concert. It would further enable her to take a third friend who would scream and enjoy it, rather than an elderly mute killjoy.

Thus it was that I found myself on the Isle of Dogs one Saturday evening, along with 11,000 young girls and a smaller number of parents in their forties. I made one final attempt to get out of the commitment. "You could sell the tickets for £100 each."

There was a moment's hesitation as that figure was converted into new items of clothing. But, in the words of the economist, the offer landed on the wrong side of her indifference curve and it was rejected. She disappeared inside, under a sea of pink hats and showing signs of incipient hysteria.

I found a Bangladeshi restaurant in the area, of which there are about three hundred. Over a meal, I dictated two days worth of constituency correspondence. My secretary reports that the enunciation became more breathless after the chicken vindaloo.

And then back to the arena, following the sound of the screams. We met at the rendez-vous and Daughter No. 2 was strangely reflective.

Yes, the concert had been excellent, but she had nothing to show for it apart from a £7 souvenir programme. Whereas she could now have had £100, had she accepted the offer....

***

The Sock

May 1990

I am not a squeamish person; true, a long time ago, I passed out when a nurse appeared with a needle to collect my donation to the National Blood Bank, but 16 years with a ringside seat for the bloodiest spectator sport available – Prime Minister's Question Time – has made a man of me.

Nonetheless, the sight of blood smeared all over the outside of a French window in the dining-room of the ancestral home took my breath away. Not just a cubic ounce or so of the stuff; but lots of it.

Close inspection of other parts of the home revealed other traces of the substance on windows, ledges – even on the leaves of some nearby trees.

Some of it was seven feet off the ground. My wife thought it might have been a Pyrennean Mountain Dog that had stubbed its toe in the dark, then knocked on the window for help. As Son No. 2 was away at University, I had no solution to offer.

To resolve the matter, we rang the local constabulary. Their response was, quite rightly, low key. Two officers came round, looked in outbuildings and shrubbery for a corpse with not a lot of blood left, found some old tennis balls but could not solve the mystery.

The response was then escalated. Two vans arrived with the mobile dog squad. They sniffed around, gave the rabbits and squirrels some exercise and then gave up. Their boss announced they were sending for the Sock.

This is not a vintage item of clothing to give fresh encouragement to the Alsatians, but the lad from Scene of Crime.

Scene of Crime arrived with the tools of his trade, modernised since the days of Sherlock Holmes. He set about scraping samples off the window and putting them in a plastic bag.

He was, by chance, a member of the Royal Society for the Protection of Birds. Within minutes, he had solved the mystery that had stumped us. Some crows with a low IQ had seen a reflection of themselves in the window. Believing it to be a rival gang, encroaching on their territory, they had attacked with vigour. They had gone on doing so, oblivious of the self-injury they were inflicting. Retreating from time to time, they had identified the same enemy at different windows and had relaunched the offensive.

We made the Sock a cup of tea, murmured our apologies and gave a donation to the RSPB.

***

Roll Up Roll Up!

June 1990

And so the season of school fêtes is with us once more. If you see someone holding in one hand a ripe coconut gushing juice from the wound it sustained on impact and, in the other, an overcooked hamburger leaking ketchup, with a Lucky Number Programme under his arm, talking with animation to the Chairman of Governors about the benefits of local management of schools and the beauty of the National Curriculum, it is your local MP putting in a spot of overtime on a Saturday afternoon.

If it is an exceptionally warm day, parents with a score to settle with the Conservative Party are allowed to throw a sponge at the local MP, with his arms in the stocks. Paid up members of the local Labour Party, known to be strong and accurate throwers, stand five feet further away. £1 for three sponges to raise funds for playground equipment.

This year's challenge has been the fancy dress competition, with two of them to judge in one day. At West Acton Infants School, where I am a Governor, an array of young talent is assembled, each defying me not to give them the first prize. I fancied the older child dressed up as Alice in Wonderland in the middle of them, but when she turned round, it was the Headmistress, explaining the rules to the entrants.

I had a professional dispute with my fellow judge. We agreed on the first three winners, but for fourth place I fancied the Man in the Moon, whereas he was taken by the single representative of that well-known trio, Three Blind Mice. I overruled him, and the Man in the Moon stepped forward to collect his voucher. The Mouse, deprived of his sight, was happily unaware of what was going on.

Warmed up by this experience at West Acton, I removed myself half a mile to West Twyford School. Again, the theme for the fancy dress competition was nursery rhymes, and my eye was caught by a delightful Little Bo Peep, with a bonnet and, for some reason, a watering can. Having declared that they were all winners really, I summoned Miss Peep to collect her prize.

Once the felicitations were complete, the photograph for the Acton Gazette taken and the booty had changed hands, she let me into a secret. She wasn't Little Bo Peep; she was Mary Mary, Quite Contrary. What, pray, did I think Little Bo Peep would be doing with a watering can?

***

Video Nasties

June 1990

Fresh from the challenge of judging fancy dress competitions in Acton, I was invited by a local government magazine to judge some videos. Town Halls produce short videos, which explain what they do with our money – apart from making videos with it. These last between five and twenty minutes each, and an award was to be made to the best. I had been asked to be one of the judges and the three of us settled down, without visible enthusiasm, with 32 score sheets and lots of coffee to watch 32 videos containing municipal propaganda.

It was an unmemorable morning. Having spent six years as a local councillor and five years as a local government minister, I had always suspected that local government was boring. After three hours of videos, I knew it.

No one knows more about local government now than the three of us. How many tons of refuse are collected each year in the City of

Westminster; how many meals on wheels are delivered in Barnsley; how many landlords serve short measures in Brighton; and how many impurities there are in the tap water in Cornwall. A never-ending series of councillors and Chief Officers, all instantly unrecognisable, merged together in a blur of municipal greyness.

After three hours, we must be approaching the end, we thought. And there, on our screen, unbelievably, we saw a man in bed with a most attractive young lady. Which local authority service was this, I asked myself? And, as important, which was the progressive local authority that made it available? Certainly not the London Borough of Ealing, under the fresh and puritanical leadership of my Conservative friends. I reached for my checklist to start marking this unusual film, keeping one eye on the action of the screen. Script? One out of ten; the couple did not have a lot to say to each other. Originality? Ten out of ten. Readily understandable by the elderly and ethnic minorities? Certainly.

After half a minute, my fellow judges and I gave up. Entertaining though it was, we could not relate it to any local authority responsibility. Recreation? Hardly. Adult education? Possibly. We turned round to ask the person in charge of the videos which progressive authority this was and what community information was being portrayed. He had gone to sleep. The video had come to an end. The TV had automatically defaulted to BBC 1. We were watching Dallas.

***

Abroad with the CPA

July 1990

By the time this column reaches your breakfast table, its author will be in Belize with John Prescott MP. Not everyone's idea of a holiday, you may think, and indeed without being disrespectful to the Member for Hull, it won't be. We will be representing our respective parties at a Commonwealth Parliamentary Conference. I had to look up Belize before I booked my flight – when I learned geography it was called British Honduras. Its capital had been rebuilt inland because the last one blew down in a hurricane.

Colleagues who had been to Belize ahead of me were not enthusiastic. "You must visit the British garrison" was their most helpful suggestion. The nurse at the medical centre looked Belize up on her chart, whistled and then opened up a jumbo pack of syringes before subjecting me to a number of indignities. The travel agent recommended taking out additional insurance and medical cover.

For 16 years, I had subscribed to the Commonwealth Parliamentary Association without ever putting in for one of its overseas trips. A combination of length of service and shortage of takers ensured that, when I did apply to represent the UK Parliament, I went to the top of the list. Wives could escort the Members, I read; but at the Member's expense. (Or possibly at the wife's expense.) A second jumbo pack of syringes was opened.

Whatever illness we come back with, it should not be rabies, typhoid, tetanus or hepatitis. The conference agenda was gloomy. "Government medical facilities will be made available to delegates and observers, if required; but the host branch will be unable to accept responsibilities for expenses incurred as a result of illnesses necessitating treatment and/or hospitalisation."

Thus it is that we pack our bags with gifts from the House of Commons for our hosts and fellow delegates, and a diplomatic brief from the Foreign and Commonwealth Office about Belize and head west to discuss Third World Debt and drugs on the South American continent.

If there is no column next week, it is because I acquired an illness which, sadly, necessitated treatment and/or hospitalisation.

The Hurricane

August 1990

At 11 at night, our genial host at the Ambergris Caye, Belize banged on our door. "The hurricane will be here in four hours," he announced, as if giving notice of the night's entertainment. "Be prepared to move to higher ground."

The topography where we were staying was that of a snooker table. The higher ground was the roof of our single storey cabin, located next to an increasingly irritable sea which was clearly the lower ground.

He pushed some literature under our door and went off to spread the news to his other guests. He must have been working out the impact of a hurricane on his profit margins. Guests in, nil. Bad. Guests out, also nil. Good. Impact on next year's bookings. Bad. Sales of liquor that evening, up. A lot. Good.

The literature told us what to do in case of a hurricane. The more promising options had already been foreclosed. Escape was impossible; access to the island where we were staying was by boat or plane.

Page 2 had a helpful chart – "Plot your Hurricane" The weather forecast on Sky gave us the location of the hurricane's eye at half-hourly intervals, together with its speed and predicted direction. We joined up the dots, heading inexorably for Ambergris Caye.

As the night wore on, Hurricane Diana changed direction and headed for the more populous beaches in Cancun, Mexico.

We left the next day and headed for home via the Bahamas. More bad news. Our old friend Diana, fickle as ever, had changed direction again and was heading east towards us. But she had been demoted. No longer was she a hurricane. Not even a tropical storm. So exhausted was she by the fling with the caballeros in Mexico that she was but a tropical depression.

Rabbit Rabbit

September 1990

For most visitors to a restaurant, the menu they are handed is a statement of the dishes which the proprietor is prepared to serve them. It is his repertory, often built up over many years, from which the customer is invited to select some items.

Not so for one of my richer friends, who is kind enough to take me, my wife and his out to dinner from time to time at places which we could not otherwise afford to go to. For him, as many a restaurateur knows to his cost, the menu is an agenda, a starting point for negotiations, a referral point for fresh radical ideas.

First, it is the basis for a quick oral examination of the staff. "I see you serve Cherry Pie; what exactly is it made of?" was a recent starter for 10. Sometimes they are more advanced. "Your pertrix aux cerises à l'aigre-doux; is the partridge from the Yorkshire Moors or the Scottish Highlands; and how did it die?" Sometimes the questions are quite incomprehensible to those of us who are neither botanists nor vets. The restaurant staff respond with tact and patience, knowing that both tips and repeat business are at stake.

Once the oral examination is over, the menu is used not as a basis for ordering dishes, but as the first step in negotiating a dish which he hopes the chef would like to cook for him. "The gougère aux foies de volaille; could I have this with a filling without the dry sherry" "I see your tomates farçies aux crevettes come with aioli; could I have this with the jambon persillé?" And so on, until the correct permutation is arrived at and the chef is set a fresh gastronomical challenge.

At the end of one meal, his wife called for her coat. The waiter went off in search of the garment but returned empty handed. "Which coat would that be, Madame?"

The rabbit-skin one, was the answer. At last the poor man, his patience exhausted by the earlier cross-questioning, saw a chance to get his own back..

"Would that be the Armenian Mottled Mountain Rabbit, suffering from mild hypothermia; the Australian Laughing Rabbit, famous for its long ears; or the Short-Coated Squirrel Rabbit, now extinct in Mexico, but still found in the mountain ranges of Guatemala?"
Touché, old man, I muttered under my breath. He got no tip from my host, but I slipped him a fiver as I left.

***

Alton Towers

September 1990

And thus the time was come to make the annual pilgrimage to Alton Towers. Adequate gold was taken to secure admission to the shrines - £25.50 for myself, Daughter No. 2 and friend of Daughter No. 2 – for one day's act of collective worship.   A sunhat and umbrella were taken to ward off the evil spirits in the sky, rumoured to haunt Staffordshire in early September.
Since I was last there, a new altar to the God of Fear had been constructed, called Thunderloop. We joined the queue of silent worshippers and shuffled forward. As we reached the point of no return, I noticed that my young companions had peeled off, overcome by terror. I was strapped into my place in a space capsule next to a bearded pilgrim from Bootle, by profession a Community Charge Registration Officer, for whom presumably anything was exciting. As we discussed the problems of keeping the register up-to-date in areas of high turnover, high turnover was exactly what happened.
We hurled forward at the speed of light, took off, looped the loop, and then went vertically up towards our Maker, as our lives flashed past. The law of gravity eventually asserted itself; we came down, looped the loop backwards and then rose towards the heavens, this time looking earthwards. The flashbacks reached about 1965 when

the ride came to an end. Our stomachs rejoined us a couple of seconds later.

We then visited the Black Hole, a creation of Satan, who was doing good business. There was no need to close the eyes as the ride took place in the dark. We went on a number of other rides, testing to the limit my head for heights.

We arrived home at dusk to be greeted by my wife, who had found some good reason for not going on the expedition. "So glad you're back" she said, in a voice indicating that some chore lay ahead. "There are some apples at the top of that tree" indicating a branch scraping the sky. "Just shin up and get the crop in."

Daughter No. 2 and I looked up at the tree, felt giddy, looked at each other and made our excuses.

Part 2

(Ministerial career under John Major)

The Handover

Column taken over by Aurelia, under the Not Sir George Young title

October 1990

The rules of collective Ministerial responsibility reach out from the chamber of the House of Commons to the columns of the Gazette. If an indignity happens to George and it is relayed, in pursuit of innocent fun, by him in this column, our constitution insists that that indignity did not just happen to him; it visited the whole administration. This could weaken the respect in which it is universally held and so it has been ruled, from the highest source, that the ink shall freeze in his pen. If he wishes to continue writing, he must lay down his post of Comptroller of the Royal Household. Naked political ambition (disguised as loyalty to the Sovereign) has won the battle over literary fame. Last week's column was his last.

But where the rules of collective ministerial responsibility wound, those of collective family responsibility shall heal. The Editor of the Gazette, when informed that there would henceforth be a blank space 10 inches by 3 inches at the top of page 2 of his paper each week, beside the five year old picture of the local MP, did some lateral thinking. He asked whether Sir George's wife would pick up the quill he had laid down. The name of Eva Peron entered the dialogue, as a potentially helpful precedent of wife succeeding husband.

I confess I have not always read George's column; on occasions, he claims to have mislaid the paper. Those are the weeks in which my friends tell me I have involuntarily featured in it. So now the opportunity to settle some old scores is too good to miss. Editor, you're on and a draft is on the kitchen table.

Some delicate negotiations will now take place to rebalance the domestic workload. If I have to write his column, he will have to perform some of the duties which I now perform. My opening bid is one column equals preparing one meal for four. If he doesn't agree, you will read all about it.

TPOs

November 1990

Like other Gazette readers who are parents, I have been following with mixed feeling and some bewilderment the events in Manchester and Rochdale – not knowing whom to believe about the sinister practices concerning child abuse alleged to have taken place. If the social workers intervene too soon, they are accused of breaking up a family. Too late and they are in the dock for negligence.

While listening to a radio programme on Stalinism in a Post-Industrial society, I saw a car from the local council draw up outside our home.

"I'm from the council." said the well-dressed young man, displaying his photo-identity card and looking around for clues.

"I understand from your neighbours that there are at least four at risk here, and that they are unusual because of their age. I have statutory powers to serve orders, but I hope that won't be necessary. We believe in co-operation rather than confrontation."

I was taken aback. Sons No. 1 and 2 have flown the nest, the latter with a little assistance to achieve take-off and with constant return flights for refuelling. If protection is needed, I need it from him. Daughter No. 1 was indeed in hospital for an operation on her foot, but her account of the injury was plausible and no mention of the At Risk Register was made by her doctor. And Daughter No. 2 was in good form when she had been tipped out at school that morning, with her homework on the causes of the First World War drafted by her father.

Even the dogs were in good condition. There were some corpses on the lawn, but they were overweight rabbits unable to run faster than a King Charles Spaniel.

My conscience was clear. But what had the neighbours been telling the council?

I invited him in. "Of course" he added "Everything that happens here can be seen from the river. And the position in the South East of

England is getting very serious. My colleagues and I are responding to telephone calls day in and day out. Quite often we are too late and only last week I arrived just in time to prevent someone taking the law into their own hands with a chainsaw and an axe."

And thus it was that the friendly Tree Preservation Officer from Windsor and Maidenhead Council presented himself, with a view to preserving for posterity a number of the older specimens on the ancestral estate.

***

The Reshuffle

December 1990

During the year, there have been some well-publicised examples of Ministers laying down the burdens of high office in order to "spend more time with their family." I join with other parliamentary wives in commending this re-ordering of priorities, even though most of the children concerned had grown beyond the stage where an extra pair of hands were needed.

However, whom did I see, fighting his way against the traffic in this one-way street of repentant husbands, but the member for Ealing Acton seeking the burden of an office, if not of a particularly high one. The children and I draw but one inescapable conclusion. He wishes to spend less time with us.

True, George rejoined the administration last July as Comptroller of the Household, but the life of a Whip – as I understand it – is intellectually undemanding. He is the head of a small family of MPs, dealing with occasional outbreaks of irreverence, ill-discipline, poverty, amnesia, ill-health, marital infidelity and unpunctuality, with an assortment of inducements, sanctions and instruments of parliamentary torture. There are also sporadic demands on his time of a ceremonial and constitutional nature, which involve putting on clothes which he does not normally wear and sometimes does not even possess; but no wife could object to that, as long as she is bought a new hat, so she can go with him to the Palace. Then I heard that he has been summoned again to No. 10.

With George, this means one of two things. He is either going to be sacked, or he is going to be promoted. Looking back at his form, as a bookmaker would, the odds are roughly evens, though he has been having a relatively good run recently. But he emerged this time with the trappings of office – a red box or two, a government car and a driver. (In 1979, on his first day as a Minister, he rang to say a black princess would be taking him home. Mercifully, this turned out to be nothing more exotic than a vehicle made by British Leyland.)

His absences from home are more noticeable and less predictable. His diary is held on a computer somewhere in Whitehall, and copies are made available to me on request. I can tell readers he will be spending less time watching Queens Park Rangers, and less time playing squash at Stripes. The former is a thinly disguised blessing, given their position near the bottom of the First Division; the latter will add an inch or two to the ministerial waistline.

Sadly, his new job will make my life as an author more difficult. He has signed the Official Secrets Act, amended since his last spell, but still a serious inhibition to indiscretion. The raw material quarried for this column will be even harder to mine.

A New Car

March 1991

George read in a Sunday newspaper that this was a good time to buy a second hand car. Each time this happens, he discovers later he got too little for the one he sold and paid too much for the one he bought, but he remains undeterred. We have a fleet of two cars, but are a family of five car drivers, all of whom believe they are entitled to a car when they need one. Three cars would give the wrong environmental signals, so one was sold to make way for a replacement.

The article in the paper said that the best bargains were cars that were nearly new and which had belonged to the senior executives of companies that had gone into liquidation (although this meant a bigger car than we normally own). We decided to back the judgement of the motoring correspondent.

George confines his major purchases to traders in the constituency in order to play his part in promoting employment and wealth in West London, and to ensure that the multiplier effect of his expenditure percolates through to local shops, pubs and restaurants. So we made our way to a large warehouse on the A40 and took with us the Chairman of the Acton Conservative Club, a man who knows a big end from a small one. My only request was that the car should be lead-free and have a catalytic converter and that its previous owner was a non-smoker. George was happy so long as it had a heater and a radio, and he could sit in it without cricking his neck.

The Chairman and George took part in a traditional tyre-kicking dance on the forecourt, followed by the ritual of the opening of the bonnet, the prayer by the boot (to inspect the exhaust) and the ceremonial haggling with the proprietor.

I have no doubt that we have a bargain. We drove it home to put in the garage. It was six inches too long. We are now looking for a second hand garage, the property of a redundant senior company executive.

Family Reunion

April 1991

And so to Oxford, to celebrate the 80th birthday of one of George's immortal aunts. The M40 from London to Birmingham is a great boon for those who live in Ealing and have relatives in Oxford who celebrate their birthdays there; so long as you see the signpost for the Oxford turnoff. Otherwise the route via Banbury is no quicker than the old A40. We arrived at the riverside restaurant late, but, owing to some genetic defect, most of the others had also missed the turnoff. In the car park there was not a foreign vehicle to be seen. The Youngs are a patriotic family.

There are many leaves on the family tree, for the tribe is a fertile one. With an average of four children per marriage, they are not exactly founder members of the World Population Movement; but, on the other hand, they tend to be monogamous. The principal concern of the older members of the family was the capacity of the family vault in the church in Cookham. After seven generations, even with the compacting offered by cremation, space is now at a premium. George, as Head of the Family and Custodian of the Vault, was taking bookings from the less robust members of the family, anxious to procure space before the "House Full" sign goes up.

A cake with 80 candles was wheeled in, with the appropriate incantation. Speeches were dispensed with, apart from the speech announcing that there would be no speeches. Then, in a display of inherited skills, many of the younger Youngs took to the river in punts – the first Sir George having been an admiral.

After two hours, I had just about identified all the new cousins I had acquired on marriage – indeed, one I had not seen since she was a bridesmaid. All, that is, but one. A brooding young man, unhappy and sitting all alone in a corner, while the revelry took place around him. Even when a glass broke, he was reluctant to join in the laughter. I saw in his eyes the despairing, hunted look of the Youngs, which I sometimes see in George's face when the opinion polls predict political oblivion.

I took pity on this young relation and approached him. He picked up a notebook at his side, as if to record my remarks. "Hello" I said "I'm George's wife. "How exactly are you related to him?"

"I'm not" he replied. "I'm the owner of the restaurant."

***

A Progressive Dinner

May 1991

When it comes to socio-political events, there is little that the Ealing Acton Conservatives can be taught by other Associations. From race-nights to bridge evenings, from winter balls to barn dances, from fancy-dress parties to cricket matches, events are laid on for every age and income group; for the athletic and sedentary; the gourmet and the diet-conscious; for the accomplished ballroom dancers, and for George. So full marks to Southfield Ward for introducing us to a novel event – The Progressive Dinner. (Food is important to the local Party – indeed, George has renamed them the Eating Acton Conservatives.)

Progressive is not, in this context, descriptive of the politics of the Southfield Ward committee, who are socially conservative. Progressive relates to the itinerant nature of the meal on offer. Apéritifs at one house; hors d'oeuvre at the next; fish at the third; main course at the fourth; dessert elsewhere; and coffee and peppermints at the final destination. A gastronomic treasure trail, with a prize at every point. Holding in one hand a list of the addresses of their hosts and, in the other, a map of the relevant polling district, a number of hungry Conservatives could be seen walking around Bedford Park one Saturday evening.

It was like canvassing, but with a difference. Instead of knocking on doors and being told to go away, one knocked and was invited in and entertained regally. However, just as one was ready for a second helping, a whistle was blown, the map and address of the next host put in one's hand, and it was back to the pavement. New hosts and new guests – for one's fellow diners also changed. The time came, around 11pm, for us all to return home. But no MP can leave a political event without a speech, setting out a coherent analysis of the political issue of the day. George cleared his throat and there was a respectful silence. He declared himself grateful for the hospitality that had been extended to him, and impressed by the itinerant nature of the evening. So impressed was he that his opening remarks would be made in the house in which he now found himself; the development of the argument would be delivered at the Church Hall of St Michael and All Angels; the examples that substantiated the argument would be declaimed in the nearby scout hut; while the peroration would take place at Southfield School. Questions would be taken in The Swan.

***

On Your Bike

July 1991

And so, with George, to Crystal Palace on the tandem, to bicycle 35 miles to Hever Castle to raise money for Friends of the Earth. Spotting our arrival, the public address system announced the presence of the Minister of State from the Department of the Environment.

This was greeted with acclamations that were more earthy than friendly. "Tories Out"; "House the Homeless"; "On Your Bike." It was the last of these injunctions that we chose to observe.

A yellow armband was securely affixed to George, to identify him to the media along the route as Someone Worth Photographing. We joined 4000 others on the pilgrimage through the streets of suburbia until we reached the hills of Kent.

I recall being taught at school that if two identical boxes are dropped from the top of the Eiffel Tower, one full of lead and the other full of feathers, they both hit the ground at the same time. I no longer believe it.

At the top of the hills, George and I would be behind a given bunch of cyclists. However as we went down, after a few hundred yards of free-wheeling, the tandem would gently overtake the others, even if they were pedalling. "It's just the gravity" we murmured apologetically, as we bowled past. When it came to going up the hills, there was no doubt whose side gravity was on. We had to dismount and we were, of course, overtaken. Not just by those still on their bikes; we were overtaken by those walking.

We looked round for our advertised fellow-celebrities – Glenda Jackson and Fatima Whitbread – but they were nowhere to be seen. Along the road, there was entertainment. A poet was declaiming sonnets. A comedian was behind a gate with a blade of grass in his mouth. "You're riding too close together" was the bon mot he had prepared for the tandem riders.

A few miles from our destination, George was in difficulty. The circulation of blood to one arm had stopped, threatening his ability to steer. I removed the yellow armband and the problem was solved, though George now blames me for the absence of any coverage of our journey in the press. We arrived at Hever Castle and handed in our sponsorship forms. We asked after Glenda and Fatima. Fatima had been called to Spain at short notice. Glenda had a conflicting environmental commitment – Saving the Whale – at a rally in Trafalgar Square. But a less energetic one; she only had to pace up and down a platform, instead of bicycling 35 miles.

***

The Body Clock

July 1991

And so to Heathrow, to meet George on his return from a Ministerial visit to Finland. He arrived tired.

His body clock prevents him from sleeping until the sun has set – some overhang from primitive man. He had gone to bed the night before at 11pm and waited for the God of Hypnos to take over. But the sophisticated control mechanism that governs his body clock was receiving clear signals from the crow's nest that the sun was still up.

The muscles that keep the eyelids open were therefore instructed to stay at their post, and the brain continued to spin round at 3000 revs, instead of ticking over. The Member for Ealing Acton lay patiently in bed, waiting for the sleep signals to turn green.

Unfortunately in Finland in June, the sun does not set and he has no override mechanism. Which is why he was tired.

I drove him to the House of Commons, where he was looking forward to a relaxing evening dining with Ealing's Head Teachers and some exchange teachers from America. He then discovered a piece of paper had been circulated to all the guests, advising them that he would be addressing them after the meal and that he was well known for his ready wit.

As the time approached for him to make his speech, the sun outside decided it was time to knock off. With the arrival of dusk, the sensing mechanism within the Minister, awaiting such a signal with growing impatience, flashed the good news around the system. Eyelid muscles relaxed; the muscles holding the head upright went off duty, the brain decelerated. As the Toastmaster prayed silence for the Honourable Member for Ealing Acton, it was abundantly clear that the wit was anything but ready.

***

A Piece of Skirt

July 1991

And so, on George's arm, to Henley to watch the rowing. Neither of us had been for some time though, as it turned out, little had changed in the intervening 30 years. With one exception; the car park.

Last time we went, the car park was used for parking cars. This time, the car park was for holding picnics.

Not the sort where anything as common as a rug was heaved out of the boot, and a chicken leg held in the hand and nibbled. But a picnic which took place in a small marquee, eaten off the finest linen with all the accoutrements of a banquet at a palace. Even, in one case, with a butler at hand. The very latest in picnic technology was on display – complete with portable televisions to save the exercise of walking 50 yards to the river to watch the races.

We had not brought a picnic and didn't feel like gatecrashing the ones in the car park. So we went on our way to the river bank to observe the Ritual of the Short Skirt. A lady in the queue in front of us was stopped at the entrance to the Stewards' Enclosure and denied admission. On asking why, she was advised that her skirt was too short. She appealed against the decision, calling in evidence a lady already inside the tent wearing a dress that was equally provocative. Her appeal was turned down, despite moral support from all the men in the queue behind her. She demanded to take the matter to a Higher Authority. An official with the responsibility of skirt length adjudicator was summoned from the tent, and he arrived, polishing his glasses.

He set about his task with relish, but without haste. The lady was examined from the front, and from the back, walking and stationary, in order to judge whether her dress was a threat to public order. Eventually, she was allowed in.

At Wimbledon, the fallibility of human judgement has been replaced by modern technology. The length of the serve is validated by sensors in the ground, linked to a computer, linked to a machine that bleeps.

The same genius is working on a machine for introduction next year at Henley. Capable of scanning thousands of thighs a minute as they walk past an electronic eye, it will bleep when too much flesh is exposed. And yet another skilled profession, that of skirt length adjudicator, will join the ranks of tinker and candlestick maker – victims of progress.

***

Revision

September 1991

We are deeply fond of Son No. 2 and nothing which follows or indeed has appeared in earlier columns should be interpreted otherwise.

We are nearly as fond of his many friends, even though they cannot make the distinction between their home and ours. But we were glad to see him and them go abroad for two weeks. Glad for them of course. We were so glad for them that we went so far as to take them to Victoria to make sure they caught the train.

Our friend, to whose cottage in France six 20 year olds have now gone, has assumed the load which has slipped from our shoulders. In theory, he has nothing to worry about. The object of the stay is to do some serious revision for the exams which confront them all at the end of their third year at University. Our friend has comprehensive household insurance should the occasional relaxation from their revision get out of hand; and there are some neighbours prepared to contact him should the need arise. And there is no telephone in his second home in France, so there is no contingent liability for calls home, or indeed elsewhere.

Although Son No. 2 is no longer with us, he has ensured he will not be far from our thoughts. A number of girl friends, not privy to his movements, have telephoned to enquire after him.

He is due home shortly and, to make him feel really welcome, I decided to spring-clean his room.

There, in a corner, was a pile of books with a note on the top. "To take on holiday for revision."

***

A Man's Best Friend

October 1991

I was woken up in the morning at 7.10 by George talking to me. Not an unusual experience for a wife perhaps, but this time he was asleep at my side. And he doesn't declaim housing statistics loudly in his sleep. His voice was in fact on the Today Programme, which had come on with the radio alarm. He had recorded the interview the night before, following a technical difficulty last time he was interviewed live in the radio car.

Two months ago, anxious to confront the Housing Minister with his Labour Shadow, the Today Programme sent the radio van down the M4 to the ancestral home. While his Shadow was in the studio in London, the van arrived in Cookham with 20 minutes to go. Having satisfied the crew that he was ready to be interviewed in the van, George returned indoors for a cup of tea and a last minute look at the statistics that supported his case.

With ten minutes to go, and the figures for housing starts and completions for the past three years fresh in his memory, George looked outside. The van had gone. We telephoned the studio who advised us that the van had been in a broadcaster's Bermuda Triangle, from which nothing could be transmitted. (We live in the valley of the Thames). The van had therefore gone in search of a stronger signal "to a nearby field" in the interests of quality broadcasting. Our house is surrounded by fields; a child was sent on to the roof with some binoculars, but a brief sweep failed to locate the van. Informally dressed in his slippers, George set out to track it down. He came across the postman. Had he, the postman, by any chance seen a three ton broadcasting van with a mast 60 feet high? Well, as matter of fact, one had caught his eye a quarter of a mile away, by the cricket pitch. George sprinted off towards it and arrived there, seconds before Brian Redhead's first question.

As George put the headphones on, there was a commotion outside. Our dog, anxious for some morning exercise, had sprinted unseen behind his master down the lane and was distressed at being separated from him outside the van. He barked very loudly, threatening the quality broadcast the sound engineer was after. There was no alternative. The door of the van was opened, the dog hauled inside and with one hand clamped over its muzzle, the interrogation on housing policy began. So, the next time the BBC wanted an interview, it was pre-recorded.

***

The Public Expenditure Round

January 1992

It being the beginning of the year in the Young household, it is time for the annual estimates. Since George rejoined the Government he has, I am afraid to say, adopted some of the stricter conventions associated with managing the Consolidated Fund. Negotiating the household budget with George resembles a bilateral discussion between the Chief Secretary of the Treasury, and the Secretary of State for a major spending department at a time of restraint.

A: "I think it's time we relaid the paving stones around the house. We could sell my BT shares to pay for it."

G: "We could sell the shares, but I am afraid only 25% can be re-invested – 75% of the proceeds must be used to pay off debt. I will of course keep this prescribed proportion under review. But it would be highly inflationary if the whole amount was spent in one year. Expenditure must be contained, no matter how it is financed; and the timing of any disposal of shares in previously publicly-owned industries is a highly sensitive matter, on which the Secretary of State for Trade and Industry has strong views."

A: "What about another holiday in Italy? We could take in some more open-air opera and bicycle round Tuscany on the tandem."

G: "With the pound near the bottom of the Exchange Rate Mechanism, it would add to pressure on the Bank of England to support it if we sold sterling and bought foreign currency. The Chancellor would find it more difficult to join the narrow band."

A: "We could let our house to some Italians to pay for the lire."

G: "The Home Secretary and I are reviewing the laws on squatting in the light of recent court decisions. Until that review is complete and the necessary amending legislation is through both Houses, landlords cannot be certain of regaining possession. The Leader of the House can give no guarantee that he can find time in the busy schedule for this Bill. And the Italians might claim diplomatic immunity."

A: "We didn't have a holiday last year. We could spend all the money we saved."

G: "The Chief Secretary is reviewing End Year Flexibility and the ability to carry forward underspends. His initial view is that if the money wasn't spent it should not have been in the budget, so there is nothing to carry forward."

A: "We must do something about Son No. 2's allowance. He's got two more terms at Exeter University and the bank won't lend him a penny more."

G: "Student support was increased last year by more than the rate of inflation. Indeed, prices have risen less fast than the Chancellor predicted at the time. Taking into account the new loan regime, students are better off in real terms than they were two years ago. Those facing hardship because of the withdrawal of housing benefit and income support can always turn to the Access Funds. And why is he down at the Kings Arms again?"

The Handkerchief

May 1992

Othello and Desdemona got into a terrible muddle over a handkerchief – what might have been a simple misunderstanding was aggravated by the malign intervention of Iago. It ended fatally, as lovers of Shakespeare's work know.

The Youngs nearly had a similar misunderstanding over the same piece of linen. Coming back from the House of Commons late one night, George noticed one of my handkerchiefs on the ground outside our second floor bedroom window. As a conscientious Minister at the Department of the Environment, he picked it up, brought it inside and put it near the washing machine. He thought no more of it until, the next night, a similar object was in the same place. His curiosity was aroused, but not his suspicion.

The third night, he was less inclined to give me the benefit of the doubt. Had Iago been there, he would have put ignoble thoughts into George's mind – was the handkerchief a signal, perhaps an inducement; or was it a warning that the House of Commons was no longer sitting? There was an entirely innocent explanation.

We have been invaded by spiders. The current climate is benign for them and, if you did not enjoy the film Arachnophobia, our home is no place for you. In the bath, in the sink – everywhere. And, in particular on the bedroom ceilings.

I don't believe in killing spiders, but Daughter No. 2 does not like them. As she is in the middle of GCSEs, her every whim has to be obeyed. So they have to be removed before she will sleep. Normally, I scoop them up and lob them out of the window. But this year the spiders are bigger and they bite. So scooping them up by hand is no longer an option and, although they are aggressive, swatting them with the colour supplement is unthinkable. So I have been scooping them up in a handkerchief. Shaking the handkerchief out does not work. Faced with the option of staying with the silk, or dropping two storeys into the night, the spider stays put. So the only solution is to lob the handkerchief out of the window, with the carnivorous arachnoid inside, and to collect the handkerchief in the morning. Going down two flight of stairs and out in a nightdress is not an option.

Unlike Othello, George has accepted his wife's version of events.

***

Ticking Off

June 1992

This week's column comes with another PG label – it is not for the squeamish. Our two dogs serve the same purpose as the country's nuclear deterrent, though at less cost. They are there to deter potential aggressors and need to be replaced at approximately 15 year intervals, if credibility is to be preserved. As with Trident, these two have never been fired in anger so we assume they have worked. Pacifists may disagree with this assumption.

In the course of their professional duties of patrolling the frontiers, our two King Charles Spaniels invited some guests back home. Ticks, acquired from some muntjac deer, with whom they had been fraternising. These ticks are, in effect, leeches. They attach themselves to the body of the dog and extract blood. Their head is below the skin, passing nutrition to their black gorged bodies above it. The dogs were covered with hundreds of these creatures, growing before our eyes.

Pulling them straight out is satisfying but does no favour to the dog. The body of the tick detaches itself, leaving the head behind. The correct technique resembles the movement required to take a blown light bulb from its socket. Push it in gently, then rotate anti-clockwise until the object is released and then remove it. Several kilowatts of tick were removed from the dogs in this way, but there was no prospect of removing them all. Some were in parts of the dog where our prying fingers were as unwelcome as the ticks.

Advice was sought from a local councillor who is a vet. "Give them some alcohol and the ticks will drop off." We opened a bottle of House of Commons whisky and poured some of the stuff down the throats of the dogs. They were pleasantly surprised, but the ticks were still there in the morning. We rang the vet to report back. The instructions had been misunderstood. It was not the dogs that should have been given the alcohol, but the ticks. We approached the dogs again with the whisky bottle. They raced towards it, sensing opening time, with tails wagging and tongues hanging out. We applied the ticks with alcohol soaked in a sponge and tried to stop the dogs licking it.

I can tell readers with dogs, ticks and whisky that the remedy works.

Lambeth Reunion

October 1992

And so to a secret destination in Lambeth that we could not reveal for reasons of security. We parked some distance from it and walked down the street. "You'll be looking for the Prime Minister's Party" said a local before we could ask him. "It's at the Vauxhall Heritage Centre. Right at the lights."

A posse of South Londoners outside indicated that a minor but acceptable leak had taken place. It was a gathering of politicians, assembled to commemorate 30 year's service on Lambeth Borough Council by Councillors Chambers and Greenwood. Guest of Honour, the member for Ferndale Ward from 1968 to 1971, Councillor John Roy Major. My political career began the same day as the Prime Minister's, though I am the first to admit that he pursued his with greater diligence and success. He, George and I were elected to Lambeth Borough Council in May 1968, much to everyone's surprise. George gave the agent my name to fight the ward we lived in, and told me about it later. Our party had not won it since 1936, he assured me. "Defeat will be a formality and more acceptable to local party morale than the alternative – namely failure to contest. Sign here; and we've found two other people who also don't want to win."

As the Returning Officer announced that I had been duly returned to represent Larkhall Ward, a part of Lambeth that had yet to be yuppified, Councillor Sir George Young was no longer to be seen. Recounts, I discovered, cannot be asked for if you have won.

The day after the election, our neighbour, who had spotted the posters in our window, enquired after our progress. "How did George do?" "He got in" I replied. "And what about you, Aurelia?" "I got in as well." "Good heavens", she said, worried about the impact this would have on our two little ones "What about the children?" "None of them were standing" I replied.

Nearly 25 years on, the team of 1968 re-assembled to pay tribute to the two colleagues who had first got elected in 1962 and had stayed on ever since, surviving both political swing and the old man with the scythe. The achievements of the Prime Minister and the Minister of State for Housing, by contrast with this display of political stamina, paled into insignificance.

YOUNG **X**

Aurelia Young

wife of Sir George Young and daughter of sculptor Oscar Nemon, is mother of two small children. She is a registered foster parent and interested in primary education. She feels strongly about bad housing conditions in Larkhall Ward, and would like to see more pre-school play groups established for the benefit of working mothers, and more open play areas for the children.

What had got the Youngs interested in municipal matters? George had been quite clear. An annual rate bill for £45 for the modest house we occupied was evidence of extravagance which only personal service on the council would redress.

We met old friends at the party, including the former Whip on the council who had had to cope with inconvenient displays of political independence by the Youngs and hadn't forgotten.

At the end of the party, after the presentations, the speeches and the raffle, someone I didn't recognise came up with a piece of paper. "Would you like to sign this nomination paper for me ? We haven't won Larkhall since you fought it in the 60's"

***

The Advice Bureau

November 1992

And so, with George, to the Old Fire Station in Acton High Street, recently refurbished to a high standard by Age Concern, for his weekly Advice Bureau. On a Saturday, we usually have the building to ourselves, though occasionally we share it with a jumble sale, a wedding or a children's tea party. Tea, champagne or orange juice is then generously offered to us, depending on the nature of the event and the age of the participants. In return, we dispense free advice, if required.

My task on Saturdays is to disengage from the wedding guests, the purchasers of second-hand clothing and the small children those who have made appointments to see the local MP and to direct them upstairs to the room where he sees them, ironically named after his Labour opponent in two General Elections, Glen Barnham.

Not all those who come know that the lady at reception is married to the man upstairs, nor is there any reason why they should. Questions such as "Do people find him easy to get on with?" and "Is he in a good mood today?" I answer as best I can. I also overhear a few asides after the interview, which I keep to myself.

On one occasion, it was clear that all was not well upstairs. Raised voices could be heard and allegations that promises made recently had been broken. An angry constituent came down the stairs and I deducted one from George's majority of 7007.

"What's the problem?" I smiled. "Plenty. He's got no size ten shoes; no winter sweaters; and no shirts. And I paid 20p to see him."

I directed him to the jumble sale downstairs.

***

Hair of the Dog

December 1992

The conflict facing the MP's wife is a recurrent one; to be by the side of her man in the constituency; or to be by the side of his children in the home. There is no simple answer and often we wives get it wrong – attending some event of mind-boggling tedium in the constituency when we could be taking the children to a good film. At other times, one is at home presiding over a squabbling family, when one could be on the tiles in W5 or W4. Or occasionally W3.

A fortnight ago, the children won and George was let loose in the constituency without an escort. When he got back, I wondered if I had made the right call. He came home with some odourless liqueur on his hands, blonde hairs on his trousers and a smell of Wembley Greyhound Stadium about him. I looked through the copy of his diary which his private office send me, to see what his alibi was. A party political function in Southfield ward, and then a visit to the Brentham Club to join the Christmas Party for members and volunteers of the Ealing Blind Club. Southfield Ward can be lively, but they would never misbehave in front of their MP. And the Ealing Blind Club is unequalled in its reputation for sobriety and respectability, as of course is the Brentham Club where they were meeting. Both functions were harmless and I knew the Mayor of Ealing was at the Brentham Club to keep an eye on the proceedings. So who was the blonde? Who spilt the odourless liqueur on his hands? And what was that smell?

I should have known better than to let a glimmer of suspicion enter my mind. At the Brentham Club, George had progressed from table to table, engaging in conversation the blind and partially-sighted members of the club. As he sat down at each table, he was greeted by the pack of golden Labradors parked underneath by their owners. He thus emerged from the Club, with canine saliva dripping from his hands, strands of golden hairs attached to his trousers and smelling as if he worked for a vet.

That at any rate is his story. I shall ask the Mayor for confirmation when I next see him.

***

Self Employment

January 1993

Having read the advice given to the Director General of the BBC by his accountant, and of the fiscal benefits of being paid through a company, I picked up the telephone and spoke to my accountant.

"I would like to incorporate myself" I told him. "Whom am I speaking to?" he asked. "Lady Young Ltd" I replied "A joint stock company owned by myself and my four children. My husband is not allowed an interest in me any more, as he is a Minister." There was a pause as he unpicked the logic of that last sentence.

"What goods and services does Lady Young provide?" he asked, reaching for his notepad and activating the clock that indicates how much he should charge me for his time.

I explained that I was a rearer of children, a supplier of hot meals to members of the Government, an opener of bazaars in the London Borough of Ealing, author of a column in a weekly newspaper and, until recently, chauffeur to a student attending a place of higher education. There was another pause, broken only by the sound of a clock ticking away the pounds the other end. "Do you choose your own hours of work? Do you have a boss? Would you describe yourself as self-employed? The Revenue are tightening up on loopholes."

"Self-employed? My children think I work for them. Do I have a boss? We have a marriage of equals here? Hours of work? Determined by the divisions in the House of Commons, the health and appetite of Daughter No. 2, and the mess left behind by her friends."

As the conversation developed, it was clear there was something important missing. A revenue stream. The goods and services supplied by the Director General of the BBC were goods and services for which DG Ltd was paid. This was a detail absent from the trading operations of Lady Young Ltd, accounting for its poor results, absence of dividends and resentful attitude of the other shareholders.

"You need to price your time and then invoice your clients – as I do with mine." he said, looking at his clock and filling in a timesheet.

I hung up.

A Night at the Opera

May 93

And so to a performance of an obscure opera by Donizetti at Covent Garden, performed by the Welsh National Opera Company on tour. Knowing that many Welsh people live in Ealing Acton, my inclination before the performance was to be complimentary about its quality in any written report. But no white lies need be told. It was superb.

The opera contains the essential ingredients of an eighteenth century tragedy.

A hero, Ferdinando, burdened with a punctilious and inconvenient sense of honour, achieves victory on the battlefield; but his engagements with the ladies are less successful.

A monarch, sardonic, sensual and corrupt; unfaithful to his beautiful and saintly wife.

A heroine, Leonora, who has lost what the librettist describes as her honour, confronted with a choice between the two men – a choice far tougher than Cilla Black gives the contestants on Blind Date.

Two important communication failures, leading to misunderstandings of tragic dimensions.

Gossiping courtiers, providing a David Coleman-like running commentary.

A marriage ceremony broken off at a crucial moment. The retirement of one of the injured parties to a monastery. Reconciliation and forgiveness, but not until too late.

And, as the curtain falls, the monks pray for the soul of she who had started out without much honour and had progressively lost more in the opera's four acts.

There was but one technical hitch. At a key point in Act 3, in the Great Hall of the Palace, our hero rejects the heroine, tears off the insignia of his nobility and then breaks his sword at the King's feet. The specification of the sword was clearly too high. Ferdinando grasped the handle in one hand, the tip in the other, and brought it down on his right thigh as he raised his foot. The sword bent, but did not break.

The audience lent forward. We had read in our programmes that this was a moment pregnant with symbolism. The renunciation of force by the young officer, after leading the Spanish Army to victory over the Moors; the end of his service with the King, whose insult to his dignity knows no bounds; a prelude to Ferdinando's return to the pacifism of the monastery.

Ferdinando tried again, but the sword remained intact. His expression had already adopted that prescribed by the librettists Messrs Jannetti and Sonzogno – one of outrage at the insolent behaviour of the King and Leonora. It was now compounded by the insolence of the sword. He tried again as the conductor instructed the drums to be kept rolling for a little longer. Finally, it snapped. The two pieces were flung defiantly at the feet of the monarch. The audience sat back and the timpanist turned over the page.

***

Pray Silence for ...

June 1993

And so to the St Ermin's Hotel for the Annual Dinner of the National Association of Estate Agents, whose health the Minister of State for Housing had been invited to propose, coupled with the name of their President.

The nation's estate agents could not have invited a less appropriate guest of honour. Having lived in the same place for over 200 years, the Youngs are not a good advertisement for the mobility that is the life-blood of the Association. Indeed, if we all moved as infrequently as the Youngs, there would never have been a National Association of Estate Agents. To compensate for coming from a family that had not spoken to an estate agent for seven generations, George was obliged to meet 170 of them all at once. And generous hosts they turned out to be.

George's after-dinner speech was sandwiched between the Band of the Grenadier Guards and the comedian Lance Perceval. This seemed unfair competition. The band were carefully rehearsed and ruthlessly disciplined. Perceval would be equally well-rehearsed but less disciplined. The former would have the audience tapping their feet; the latter would have them holding their sides. What would be their response to the Minister?

George had taken delivery in his red box the night before of a speech of mind-numbing tedium, drafted by his Department. It began with the Property Misdescriptions Act, moved on to the Index of House Prices published by the Nationwide and Halifax Building Societies; and climaxed with an announcement about the Chief Land Registrar and a National Land Information System.

Discretion is often the better part of valour. Sensing the mood of the evening, George decided to downsize the speech and spice it up with some jokes of his own. Major surgery took place over the pudding, with chunks of the speech being excised. The Chief Land Registrar was an important casualty. George handed over the discarded sections to the Toastmaster for disposal.

The Toastmaster, a man whose profession obliged him to listen with rapt attention to Ministerial orations, however boring, glanced with relief at the excised pages. "A very wise decision, if I may say so, Sir George. They will want to get back to the bar." George looked far happier with what was left.

As the Toastmaster was about to pray silence for the Rt Honourable Sir George Young, Minister of State at the Department of the Environment and one of Her Majesty's Privy Councillors, the President told George that his Department had released the text of his unexpurgated speech to the Press, who would publish it in full the next day; and that he, the President would be basing his reply on behalf of the guests to the key points in that speech, of which the Department had kindly sent him an advance copy. He wanted, in particular, to respond to the promised announcement about the Chief Land Registrar.

Nothing to Declare

June 1993

And so to Terminal 3 at Heathrow, to collect George from his flight back from Beirut. Every Minister has to do his bit to promote exports and George has responsibility for the construction industry. So he had taken soundings from the country's civil engineers to see where he could best help them win export orders. He double-checked with the DTI and the Foreign Office; and the answer was the Lebanon.

As he left, three days earlier, he had assured me there was no need for concern since he knew Beirut. He had grown up there. On cross-examination, it turned out he had spent six months there when he was three. As there had subsequently been sustained military action, including a civil war lasting 17 years that had flattened the centre of the capital, it seemed unlikely that any childhood memories would be evoked as he wandered around. It also turned out that he had started his formal education there. As the school was a French one for five year olds and George's English, let alone his French, was poorly developed at the time, he must have been a real nuisance.

When the plane landed back at Heathrow, it disgorged the Minister and the team of export-hungry entrepreneurs he had taken with him. The event that stuck in George's mind was not one that took place in the bustling bazaars of the Middle East, nor in the diplomatic exchanges with his Ministerial counterparts. It took place in the clinical surroundings of the Customs Hall of Terminal 3. A lady of stunning beauty and figure marched through the Red Channel and accosted the official of Her Majesty's Customs and Excise, who was on duty. "I have absolutely nothing to declare" she informed him.

"Nothing to declare? Then madam is in the wrong channel. The Red Channel is for those who have acquired goods to the value of £30 or more during their stay abroad. The Green Channel is for those, like madam, within the permitted limits."

Which, being interpreted, means "Are you colour-blind or what?"

"I'm coming through this channel on purpose" she replied. "Whenever I go through the Green Channel with nothing to declare, I'm challenged, interrogated and searched by your colleagues. It takes 30 minutes and I am a busy person. If I come through this channel, I get rebuked for wasting time and then waved through."

There was a pause while the servant of the crown looked at the goddess, digested this information, and surveyed the growing queue of people behind her, with goods to declare. "Be on your way, and don't waste my time again." Her bluff had worked.

**

The Raffle

September 1993

"No, I'm sorry, George isn't in. This is his wife. Can I help?"

"The Secretary of the Acton Vegetable Growers Association? Yes, of course. Hallo. How kind of you to phone, George is thrilled at being your Patron. And he so much enjoyed his visit last Sunday to the Autumn Show – what a good picture of him and Madam President's marrows in the Gazette, though I found the caption a bit risqué."

"No, we haven't eaten all the 18 which she gave him just yet. If you have any interesting recipes, we'd be pleased to try them out. I'm running out of ideas."

"Yes, I know he bought some raffle tickets. I found them in his trouser pocket when I took the suit to the cleaners. ...He won something? He'll be so pleased."

"The five foot pink teddy bear that plays "Home Sweet Home" when you hug it? He'll be ecstatic."

"No, it sounds as if it won't fit on the back of his bike. I'll pop round tomorrow afternoon and collect it in the car. Just remind me of your address."

A few moments later.

"No, I'm sorry, George isn't in. This is his wife. Can I help?"

"The Secretary of the Ealing Branch for Country Dancing? Yes, of course. Hallo. How kind of you to phone, George is thrilled at being your Patron. And I know how much he loved joining in the action after your AGM."

"Yes, his back has recovered from the collision during the Cumberland Square – was the Chairman's wife badly concussed?"

"I'm so glad. You're having another party this Friday? What a shame – we'll be in Blackpool at the Party Conference."

"Yes, of course I'll pass on to him your very frank assessment of his party's performance. Tell me, are you having a raffle?"

"Good. George would very much like to contribute a prize to help raise funds"

"No. I think I'll leave that as a surprise for you. It's quite big. Just remind me of your address and I'll bring it round in the car tomorrow afternoon."

***

Fancy Dress

November 1993

The invitation to Son No. 2 was explicit. He was invited to attend the 21st Birthday Party of a contemporary, but on condition he came dressed up as an angel. His host had gone to some trouble to secure diversity of apparel amongst the guests. Other friends had been invited to attend disguised as bears, nuns, clowns and a variety of anthropomorphic characters from the nation's favourite pantomimes. Why he was allotted the role of an angel was a mystery, but it was going to be cheaper than dressing him up as Godzilla.

The family dressing-up box was of little use as he is now twice as tall as when he last used it. He was despatched to go and buy some angel wings, while work at home commenced on the halo. Readers may have made a halo, using a wire coat hanger and a round baking tin with the centre removed. It was low-tech – the type of project a primary school teacher might have given her class. We perched it on his head, draped a sheet over him, and then affixed the wings to his back. While it was unlikely to deceive St Peter, we felt it would qualify for admission to the party.

We folded him carefully into the car and then drove off to pick up Red Riding Hood, Dick Whittington's cat and a wolf. Halfway to the party, the cat looked at the invitation to check the address and saw that they were all expected to bring a bottle. None of them had got one.

I stopped at the Off-Licence and made it clear that I was not going to do the buying. There was a lively discussion as to which of them was going inside to make the necessary purchases. The wolf said he couldn't get the money out of his pocket without undressing in the shop. Red Riding Hood had gone to some trouble to be conspicuously under age. The cat said that Dick Whittington was the one with the cash. In the end, they all went in.

The temptation to drive off and leave them to explain themselves to the other punters in the shop was almost irresistible.

Disconnected

January 1994

Most of us have insurance of some sort. And, when disaster strikes, the blow is softened by the warm embrace of our insurance company wrapping itself around us. Unless of course it turns out that the configuration of the particular disaster matches one of the exclusion clauses in small print at the end of the contract. The embrace is abandoned and one is alone.

One minor disaster against which the Youngs have insured themselves is social isolation – being cut off from the rest of the world through discontinuity in the telephone service. To minimise the damage done by such a discontinuity, we have subscribed since 1986 to British Telecom's Total Care Scheme. When we started, it cost £10.45 per quarter but now, doubtless after securing the concurrence from the folk at OFTEL, it is £18.90, to which VAT must be added. This offers "a guaranteed fast response to reported faults." The literature summed it all up. "If your phone is vital to you and you can't afford to be without it, then Total Care is right for you."

The major benefit, the literature tells us, is that "our engineers will respond to any fault which might occur within four hours – we guarantee it. That's any time of the day or night, every single day of the year."

And for seven years we have paid – sleeping secure that, in the event of disconnection, the heroes from British Telecom will overcome technical and physical problems to reconnect us again. Last month, it happened. I picked up the phone and it was silent. George tried it and, with the experience of having worked for BT for four years before becoming an MP, pronounced life extinct. We commandeered a neighbour's phone and rang in, quoting our Total Care reference, reminding them that it was right for us. We sat back, visualising a team of engineers climbing telegraph poles, opening junction boxes, peering along ducts while the supervisor watched the minute hand on a stopwatch. The service was, after all, "backed by all the resources and professionalism of the leading telecommunications company in the UK."

Four hours later, we were still isolated; indeed, 40 hours later, we were still without service. I rang in from the tolerant neighbour, with the Total Care leaflet in my quivering hand, asking what might have happened to the professionalism of the UK's leading telecommunications company.

"Ah" I was told "We say our engineers will respond within four hours; and they did. But we don't say that they will restore service."

And it is the politicians who are accused of wriggling out of promises.

***

Bats

August 1994

Last night, the contents of the house were worth a million pounds; but in the morning, they had all gone – gone, as it were, with the wind. Before our insurance broker telephones for the loss adjuster, he should read on. "With the wind" gives the alert reader the clue he or she needs.

Yes, we are hosts to a colony of bats. We reckon there are over 200 uninvited guests in our home. We deduce the monetary value of our tenants by multiplying their number by the maximum penalty for molesting a bat under the 1981 Wildlife and Countryside Act. This is £5000 per beast. Two hundred times five thousand gives us the notional value of our colony. I don't know how many bat millionaires there are, but it is a status one cannot shake off. In the dull prose of the parliamentary draughtsman, any unlicensed person who intentionally kills, injures or handles a wild bat is exposed to the maximum penalty of £5000. The penalty applies equally to disturbing a roosting bat, and damaging, destroying or obstructing access to a roost. So there you are. I thought George had ended protected tenancies in the 1988 Housing Act, but I was wrong. These tenants pay not a penny in rent, controlled or otherwise, and they can pass the tenancy on to the next generation. Not just once, as under the aforesaid Housing Act, but indefinitely.

It is a compliment, I suppose, that our home should have been chosen from the many that are available. The bat is a choosy guest, going for the modern home with the cavity wall, owned by someone familiar with the 1981 Wildlife and Countryside Act and intimidated by its penalties. While we are not overjoyed by the company we have to keep, we will honour our side of the bargain. But we have an issue with their personal habits. Those droppings. In the flower beds please, and not on the window sills. A few extra seconds of bowel control is all we ask for.

***

Spiders

September 1994

And so, on the last leg of our eight day holiday, to Verona from Venice by train. It can't be much of a life; throwing large black spiders against the outside wall of a shop in Verona and watching them slither to the ground. At the same time that the octopods are projected, the perpetrators of this inhuman act need to keep an eye out for the Carabinieri; not because of any offence against the Cruelty to Animals Act, but because our culprits were street traders.

RSPCA readers will be relieved to know that the spiders were made of plastic. When thrown against a wall, they first stuck to it, and then crawled down, legs following body following legs with commendable realism.

The tourists in Verona either hurried past, if they were allergic to spiders; or stayed and watched if they were not. Every now and then, as the Carabinieri approached, the spiders were stuffed into a bag and the street traders disappeared. When the coast was clear, they would return and resume the assault on the wall with the battery of arachnoids.

We sat there watching from a nearby café. A Veronese crawling spider costs 3000 lire (£1.20) and they sold one every five minutes. Potential purchasers were given a spider, invited to throw it against a wall, and watch it crawl down. The most lucrative segment of the market is boys around the age of 12. Old enough to have 3000 lire without having to ask their parents, and possessing arachnophobic teachers or sisters. Old enough to have the necessary independence, but not old enough to have developed resistance to pavement salesmen in Italy.

My advice to readers is "Don't Buy". When no one was looking, our traders would spread the wall with some barely visible paste, which gave the spider its saleable characteristics. When the 12 year olds throw their spider against the kitchen wall at home, they will be disappointed. It will drop lifeless to the floor.

But if our juvenile punter has lost £1.20, he will have learned one of the lessons of life; a lesson which will stand him in good stead later, when the stakes are higher, with double glazing salesmen and others.

Readers' Letters

April 1993

Dear Sir

I can't understand why you give prominent space in an otherwise serious local newspaper to the incoherent ramblings of the wife of one of our local MPs. Clearly, she should be devoting her energies to the upbringing of her delinquent children and to persuading her misguided husband to abandon policies which are bringing this country and his constituents to their knees.

Yours sincerely, Disgusted of W3.

Dear Sir

Three weeks ago, you failed to publish the Not Sir George Young column. I demand reimbursement of 30p, as this is the only item worth reading in the catalogue of misery and disaster which otherwise fills your pages. It is a ray of sunshine on an otherwise overcast day.

Yours sincerely, Disappointed of W4.

Dear Sir

The domestic crises of Lady Young, taking place against her privileged background, should evoke no sympathy from your readers. In the meritocratic society which I and my comrades promote, there is simply no place for these survivors of a discredited social system, who owe their status to their parents or their partners. I demand equal space for the Workers Revolutionary Party.

Yours in brotherhood, Angry of NW10.

Dear Sir

In a hundred years time, the writings of Lady Young in an obscure West London weekly paper will be seen as the accepted social comment on the last decade of the 20th century. She writes with the observation and eye for detail of Charles Dickens; with the wit of

Oscar Wilde; and the insight of Jane Austen. The National Curriculum will surely find a place for these jewels of literary adornment.

Yours sincerely, Delighted of W5

Dear Sir

I was a staunch member of the local Conservative Party until Lady Young started writing in the Gazette. Now, I can no longer support a party whose elected representatives marry such witless creatures. How can Ministers take sensible decisions if their food is burnt, their gardens untended and their shirts unironed? My vote goes to any candidate whose domestic arrangements exhibit some order and discipline.

Yours sincerely, Dejected of W3.

Dear Sir

I think Lady Young has had a raw deal in your letters page over the past few weeks. She has been unfairly criticised for a whole range of incidents which are not her fault at all. I think her column is ghosted by her husband.

Yours sincerely, Sherlock Holmes.

**

The Last Word

July 1995

And so, Dear Reader, Farewell – for this is the last column. After nine years, it is time for the Youngs to withdraw from this space in the Gazette. Hopefully, I do so when people say "Why are you stopping?", rather than later when people say "Why did you go on?"

There are a number of reasons for drawing stumps. The column is scoured each week for stories that can be distorted and then sold to the gossip columns of the national press. This inhibits the author if she shows restraint in what she writes, and embarrasses her or her family if there is no restraint. And, to be honest, a small cloud hangs over every Sunday until the column is written.

And, after a column every week for nine years, inspiration sometimes runs dry. The column started off as George's. When his promotion made this impossible – rules expressly prevent Ministers from writing regular columns in their local press – he did what many husbands do; put the asset in his wife's name.

The news of the discontinuation of the column will bring relief in some quarters. There is a reader who meticulously corrects any errors and then sends the amended column to me anonymously with a suitable rebuke. I am grateful to him. On the assumption that what replaces this column will be of sounder grammatical construction, he will be spared distress. My family will also rejoice at the column's demise. Born into public life, they accept the inevitability of some media intrusion and exposure. ("MP's son hit by snowball" was the headline once in our local paper). But they don't see why this should come from their mother, who has more access to their private lives than a journalist.

Before signing off, I owe it to the reader to give a final bulletin on the many characters who have appeared in the column over the years. The bats are still happily living in the roof, evacuating their tiny bowels all over the windows every evening. The dogs, free of ticks, are on permanent burglar alert. The rabbits are making territorial gains on the lawn, having dug under the primary defences. The muntjacs continue to swim across the river, to graze on my plants and shrubs.

Daughter No. 2 has secured a place at Bournemouth University, and is engaged in negotiations with a former Treasury Minister about her allowance; and with a current Transport Minister about solutions to her mobility – a bicycle in his view, a car in hers.

And so, as the sun sets, and a solitary oarsman sculls up the Thames, and the cry of the wood pigeon echoes around the valley, I finally lay down my pen....

Part 3

(Years in Opposition)

The column was recommenced in my name after I became the MP for North West Hants in 1997.

The Pirates of Penzance

December 1999

The pubs in North Hampshire are not without initiative, and they promote trade in a variety of ways. Pub Quizzes, Live Music, Curry Evenings, Karaoke. Over the Christmas holidays, our local pub advertised a fancy dress evening. The theme was the Pirates of Penzance. Customers were challenged to respond by dressing up as pirates, as members of the Cornish Constabulary, or as the daughters of Major General Stanley. Those with good bass voices in the village could be heard rehearsing some of the better known choruses – "With Catlike Tread", "When Constabulary Duty" etc, and an ambitious soprano tried "Poor Wandering One" in her garden, but gave up when she reached the taxing high notes in "Take Heart" and the neighbours protested.

When the day of the fancy dress evening arrived, one of the elderly residents was unaware of the fixture. Looking out from behind her net curtain, she espied a man with an eye-patch, bearing a lethal looking cutlass, removing a camcorder from the boot of a car in the pub car park. Unhesitatingly, she dialled 999.

Meanwhile, proceedings in the White Hart were well underway. The Pirates of North Hampshire quaffed their beer or their rum, and propositioned the nubile daughters of the Major General. Suddenly, the door of the pub burst open, and in rushed a number of policemen looking for a man with a cutlass and an eyepatch who had stolen a camcorder. As they were confronted with a large number of men with cutlasses and eyepatches, they were bemused.

There was a moment of silence; and then spontaneous applause from the regulars for the authenticity of the uniforms of the recently arrived guests at the fancy dress evening.

Pensioned off

January 2000

A few weeks ago, a letter arrived from the Department of Work and Pensions, the re-badged Department of Social Security. The present Government and the previous one had apparently been dilatory about telling people of a change in the law, reducing the entitlement of a widow to inherit part of her husband's retirement pension. If I filled in the form, I would be told how much Lady Young would get if I was, sadly, knocked off my bicycle.

I filled in the form and sent it off to Long Benton. There was a delay of a few weeks before the answer came back. It was deeply disturbing. I didn't exist. "Unfortunately, we do not have enough information… We might not have your correct name, or date of birth, or contributions record, or your National Insurance records may be incorrect."

Let us pause here. There is no dispute about my date of birth, which is generously acknowledged by the Times and other quality newspapers on every anniversary of that happy event. I have had the same National Insurance number for nearly forty years (though I suppose, due to the pervasiveness of fraud, I may now be sharing it with others); and my employer for nearly 30 years, the House of Commons, has to my certain knowledge, been making appropriate and ever growing contributions to the Consolidated Fund.

That leaves us with the name. Well, it has changed, but only in the sense that a Christmas tree changes when it is decorated. When my father died, it acquired three extra letters at the front and two short ones at the end; and other baubles have been added as my modest contributions to political life have been recognised. But the core "George Young" has remained at the heart of the enterprise and the computer at Long Benton should not have been blinded by aristocratic or meritocratic sand.

But no, I was no longer there. Then another letter arrived.

"Dear Mr Young, I am sorry that we cannot provide you with an estimate of the amount of SERPS you can pass on to your spouse. But, if you fill in the form, we will tell you about your own SERPS pension in your retirement pension forecast."

Readers will have spotted the question I asked myself. If I don't exist for the purposes of passing on a pension to my widow, how might I exist for the purpose of claiming a pension for myself?

The Lottery

February 2000

I need my readers' help; somewhere in North West Hampshire, a shop has been designated a "National Lottery Community Outlet" and Camelot won't tell me where.

Let me explain. In my postbag every day are letters from people called Government Relations Managers. These are well-paid people in the private sector, whose job it is to enlist the support of Members of Parliament for whatever product or service their client is selling. The letter pays tribute to the hard-work of the local MP in some particular field, explains how the company has exactly the right product/service to meet the needs of the constituents; and suggests a lunch with the aforesaid Government Relations Manager at some congenial watering-hole near Westminster. Most go straight into the waste paper basket.

A letter dated September 20th which arrived from the Government Relations Manager from Camelot Group plc escaped this fate. It brought welcome news. "I am pleased to advise that a National Lottery retailer in your constituency has recently been designated a National Lottery 'Community Outlet'."

As I was told that "the identification of Community Outlets plays a significant role in maximising the returns to the Good Causes whilst maintaining accessibility to the National Lottery", I wanted to visit the outlet, accompanied hopefully by the diligent photographer from the local paper, and so play my part in keeping the show on the road. The letter ended with a warning that, if sales don't exceed a given amount, "terminals may be relocated to another outlet."

I wrote on September 26th to the Government Relations Manager asking for details. Where was this enterprising shop that had recently received this accolade?

There was a long delay, during which time the winning ticket I might have bought from the outlet missed three Saturday draws. And then the reply arrived in a letter dated October 21st. I quote from the letter, because otherwise you might not believe the message it contained.

"Unfortunately, as a result of the Data Protection Act, I am unable to provide further details of the Community Outlet mentioned in my letter of 20 September."

***

TV Licence

April 2000

The survival of the Post Office at Sherborne St John in the constituency featured in the local paper. This was the result of successful community action. Instead of protesting and asking someone else to do something, the village mobilised its own resources to provide the bridging finance to enable the new owners to move in. Every MP must wish he had a Sherborne St John in his or her constituency, with its capacity to solve its own problems. (Might the villagers even be able to run the nearby Atomic Weapons Establishment at Aldermaston?)

One of the products on sale at the village Post Office is a TV Licence, sales of which are accelerated by the presence of TV detector vans in the area. Many of these, as I know from the time when I worked for the Post Office in the 1970s, have nothing inside them apart from the driver's lunch and a copy of the Mirror.

Some time ago, as one such van pulled up outside a house in Tadley, the husband - who was going out to work - called out to the occupant of the van. "Don't bother to call here. I bought a licence yesterday - it's behind the clock on the mantelpiece." And with that, he left the scene.

Ever anxious to secure revenue for the BBC and distrustful of the householder's assurance, the detector knocked at the door. The wife answered it.

"I believe you have a TV set on the premises madam, and our recent records show no licence. Do you have one?" he asked, in interrogatory mode.

"Why yes, Tom went out and bought one yesterday."

"Can I see it?"

She disappeared inside, and returned empty-handed a few minutes later. "I can't think where Tom has put it."

The man returned to the van, consulted his conscience and then knocked again at the door. "Try looking behind the clock on the mantelpiece."

She returned, waving as Chamberlain did on his return from Munich, a piece of paper.

"Goodness me, how clever you are" she declared "I had no idea those detectors were so sensitive."

***

Can I count on your Support?

April 2000

Over the past few weeks, I have spent some time canvassing for my party's candidates in the local elections in Tadley, Baughurst, Kingsclere and Oakley. Nearly everyone is courteous to those of us in pursuit of votes when we interrupt the cooking, the gardening, the favourite TV programmes or, in one case, catching a mouse in the bathroom. Shiftworkers catching up on their sleep are the ones that have the most difficulty in engaging in this democratic process.

I recall my first campaign in 1968 when I was standing for the local council in Lambeth. The tree-lined street where I was canvassing was disfigured by an abandoned car with no wheels. The first household I called on, when prompted to name a local issue on which the energy of the young candidate might be applied, pointed at the vehicle. "Get that shifted and you've got my vote." His neighbour expressed similar concern and, as I moved from door to door, I could sense a tidal wave of support for cleaning up the streets. I came to the last house. "Good evening, I'm George Young, your Conservative candidate in Thursday's local election. I cannot tell you how strongly I feel about abandoned cars polluting this delightful neighbourhood. My first action on getting to the Town Hall on Friday morning, if elected, will be to mobilise the Environmental Health Department to remove this wreck, have it scrapped and send the bill to the irresponsible owner."

There was a pause while the householder looked at this pompous young man and regained his composure. "That is a 1957 Mark Seven Jaguar which I am having restored at great expense. The new wheels arrive tomorrow. You touch it, you interfering busybody, and I'll have your guts for garters."

***

The Duck Race

June 2000

And so to Westminster Bridge, to take part in the Annual Parliamentary Duck Race, sponsored by Thames Water. MPs who enter this contest present themselves to the lady from Thames Water, who allocates the Member a large yellow plastic duck with a black number on its back.

At a given moment, these ducks are hurled into the Thames to float up past the Houses of Parliament with the tide. An employee of Thames Water with keen eyesight and no political leanings is located at the winning post at the far end of the House of Lords Terrace. He identifies the winning duck, whose owner wins some money for a nominated charity of his or her choice.

I have lived or worked near the Thames nearly all my life. Three years at County Hall, gazing out on the river. Twenty-six years at the House of Commons, gazing out on the river – when not working for my constituents. Five years at Eton College, three at Oxford.

I have observed that the river does not flow evenly. There are eddies and currents, and the wind adds further unpredictability. While the colleagues were talking to each other, I was staring intently into the muddy waters below, analysing the flows. "Don't jump, George" called a friend.

Yes, one section of the river appeared to be moving faster than the others. We had to wait for a boatload of tourists to pass before we started, otherwise they would have been bombed by 50 plastic ducks, launched by the country's legislators.

At the off, my duck was hurled into a commanding lead and stayed ahead for as far as the eye could see. We repaired inside to await the result.

My duck came fourth, beaten by the one owned by the Minister for Sport. My request for a urine test on the winning three ducks was turned down. But I won £500 to share between Andover MIND and Andover Mencap.

***

Can I quote you?

September 2000

It was a pleasure to go to Kingsclere a few days ago to open the skate ramp, commissioned by the far-sighted Parish Council. These occasions contain their risks, as the local press want an action picture, hopefully of the local MP, arms outstretched, travelling at speed on wheels in a hemicycle made of concrete, displaying rare skills of equilibrium; or, scoop of scoops, legs outstretched, having taken a parliamentary tumble.

Twenty six years in the House have taught me to be cautious about posing for the Press.

As Transport Secretary, I was invited by a civil engineering company to witness progress on the construction of the Southern Derby Relief Road, doubtless a key part of my integrated transport strategy. I went to the East Midlands by train, and was driven to a muddy field to the south of the City, occupied by slow-moving contractor's traffic. I was ushered into a hut on site, where three walls were decorated, in accordance with the best of traditions of the construction industry, with scantily clad ladies. On the fourth wall was a large scale map of the new road, showing a few villages along the route. "Just to orient myself" I said, looking at the map, "where exactly is Derby?" The photographer captured my jabbing finger, and his accomplice, the local reporter, took great interest in this harmless exchange. The chartered surveyor in charge of the visit pointed to a place near the light bulb, to indicate where the City was. We went to look at the embryonic road; I sat on a dump truck; I put on a hard hat; I examined the freshly laid surface, but the hounds from the local paper were not interested in these photo opportunities. I returned to London.

My office acquired a copy of the local paper. In bold headlines across the front page was the question "Where is Derby? asks Transport Secretary".

The Way of the Lord

October 2000

One of the pleasant tasks I set myself on adoption as the prospective Conservative candidate for NW Hants was to visit every church, school and pub in the constituency. Moral and intellectual refreshment to be complemented by physical refreshment. Faster progress is being made with the pubs than the schools and churches, principally because the pubs are open for business more often. (I only go to a church when there is a service – usually on a Sunday. The pubs hold their services twice a day.) About five churches remain on the list, including one in Tadley that has just closed for the winter.

I visited my first church in the constituency nearly five years ago, when I was Secretary of State for Transport. I sat discreetly at the back, behind a pillar. The Vicar chose as his text a passage from the first lesson, Isaiah 40. "Prepare ye the way of the Lord,   make straight in the desert a highway for our God."

He then addressed himself to the moral issues raised by the building of the nearby Newbury Bypass, one of my then Department's more controversial civil engineering projects which was being obstructed by Swampy, encamped with his followers in trees along the route. The Vicar made it clear that the project was constructed on dubious moral foundations. A highway in the desert for the Almighty, advocated by the prophet Isaiah, was one thing; a highway through verdant Hampshire for his sinful followers, promoted by the Transport Secretary, quite another. I made sure I stayed behind the pillar for fear of provoking him. While he did not carry all the congregation with him – most had come to church on four wheels and nearly all would use the bypass once constructed - it was a powerful oratorical performance.

At the end of the service, we queued up to pay our respects to the Vicar. The Churchwarden ahead of me in the queue asked the Vicar, whether he knew, when he drafted his sermon, that it would be listened to with interest by the Secretary of State for Transport, who had just moved into his parish. The colour drained temporarily from the cleric's face. "No" he confessed. However, recovering quickly, he added "But the Almighty did."

***

The Whole Tooth

December 2000

At Oxford some thirty years ago, I remember introducing a guest speaker to the Oxford Union. He was a distinguished elderly gentleman, who had succeeded in the world of commerce. "We are pleased to see Mr X with us tonight" I declaimed. "He is very old and very rich. In fact, he has two dentists; one for each tooth." Mr X had the sense to laugh – not least because it displayed the falsity of my claim about his dental virility.

I am neither as old nor as rich as he. But I have two dentists. One performs the task of the jobbing builder, responding to erosion, subsidence, and decay. The other resembles the civil engineer who deals with excavation and underpinning. One concentrates on what is above the surface, enjoying the freedom of the open space. The other, like a mole, is more at home in the subterranean.

Both are high quality professionals and fully paid up members of the human race. I say that not only because it is true; but because I see from my diary that I have a number of engagements with them in the near future. "I happened to be surfing the internet, Sir George and I read this column about your dentist.. Oh, I'm sorry; did that hurt? I thought that tooth was dead…"

They work in perfect partnership, Dentist A invading a dental Hades and bringing it to order; Dentist B then constructing dental monuments for me to flash at Jeremy Paxman and a million viewers.

And so it was last week. Dentist A had excavated. The site had been disinfected, lined, cleaned and then blow-dried. For all I know, Dentist A had inscribed his initials on the wall. He then inserted a temporary tooth, in due course to be replaced by a listed building crafted by Dentist B.

I asked him about the robustness of this temporary structure, and was advised that, so long as I avoided apples and toffee, it was fit for purpose.

I took my leave, and resumed my constituency duties. I visited a flour mill in Andover and a pre-school playgroup in Overton. What my hosts made of my conversation I know not, as half my mouth was still deep-frozen.

At lunchtime, I popped in to a pub, and demanded the sandwich with the softest filling. This was delivered to my table, with an eighth of a tomato, three thin slices of cucumber, a sprinkling of cress and a paper napkin. I consumed the sandwich carefully, and felt something hard against my tongue. "Lucky I felt that" I said to myself, "It could have done injury to the tooth". In fact, it couldn't, because it was the tooth, instantly rejected by the gum.

I put it carefully in the paper napkin, and finished the meal. I drove off, wondering which of the two dentists was most likely to repair the damage. He that I had last seen, but who had given me an architect's certificate certifying completion; or he who was going to put in a new one. While I was working this out, I remembered what I had forgotten. The paper napkin, nestling on the plate next to two unconsumed cucumber slices.

Have you ever asked a pub landlady if you can look through her dustbin?

***

Hullo Hullo

September 2001

And so to the local Police Station, to spend six hours on patrol with the local constabulary to see how they maintain law and order in the constituency. And mightily impressive it was too; we were summoned to a house where the owner was building an extension. He was doing the excavation himself and unearthed what he thought was a landmine. Our intrepid policeman inspected it at close quarters, took the view that it was a discarded piece of ironmongery and kicked it to convince us of his opinion. Some of this story was received at second hand, as I chose to locate myself behind a tree while our hero defused, as it were, the situation. Then it was off to an armed robbery, with instructions for the MP to stay in the car and not become a local hero by rugger-tackling men with masks.

The last time I went on patrol with the police was when I was an inner city MP in London. The Chief Superintendent informed me that the best time to go out in the patrol car was about 10.30 the following Friday evening. We were dining with friends that night and I arranged to be collected from their home, and delivered to my own home after our duties were completed.

As we sipped coffee, my hosts were surprised when a police car screeched to a halt outside, blue lights flashing. Two policemen rushed in, removed the local MP and bundled him into the car. The police were on their way to a call, and had made a short, swift diversion to collect me for the assignment. After my departure, my wife sought to reassure our hosts and the other guests that I was not wanted to assist police in any inquiries.

I spent an interesting evening in West London, listening to the calls on the police radio, looking at nightclubs, going round the less salubrious estates looking out for people who should be arrested. It was more Z Cars than Starsky and Hutch. At about 11pm, a chilling message was broadcast to all units.

"Calling all mobiles, calling all mobiles. Which one of you has the local MP in the back? He's gone off with his car keys, leaving his wife stranded at a dinner party where the folk want to go to bed."

The Budget

December 2004

As I sat in my place listening to Gordon Brown's Pre-Budget Statement last week, I was reminded of the undergraduate's essay which began "When the artist woke up in the morning, the sunshine streamed in through the window. He felt rosy all over." His English Tutor had relieved the tedium of marking essays by scribbling in the margin "Lucky Rosy."

And so it was with the Chancellor. Prudence had left, and Rosy had arrived.

All the other economic commentators were out of step; the prospects for the economy were set fair, and all who disagreed would be proved wrong, as Gordon asserted they had been for the past eight years.

Then he said something that I thought I must have misheard. So I waited until Hansard came out the next day and read the official record. And there it was.

"We will build on successful experience by also locating employment advisers in GP's surgeries."

Hang on a minute, the sketch-writers are going to have fun with that one, I said. Put yourself in the shoes of a punter who wakes up feeling at death's door, and resolves to go to the Medical Centre to see his friendly GP to get relief. He arrives, feeling fragile and looking forward to an audience with a sympathetic health professional who will prescribe some appropriate purgative. He will take the note to the apothecary for dispensation. The apothecary will look at the customer over his horn-rimmed spectacles, purse his lips in disapproval of the lifestyle that had generated the complaint, and retreat into the bowels of the pharmacy to get the pills. And the next day, all is well.

But that is not what is apparently going to happen. On arrival at the Medical Centre, the patient does not find a benign member of the Royal College of General Practitioners. Instead, at the behest of the

Chancellor of the Exchequer, at the check-in desk is a representative from the Job Centre, eager to find shelf-stackers for the local supermarket; or possibly to discourage the issuance of sick-notes that will aggravate the Chancellor's Budget deficit.

Now, don't get me wrong. I am all for joined-up Government; for helping back into work vulnerable folk who have been marginalised and who need advice and encouragement. And no-one is in favour of scroungers.

But the Medical Centres in Hampshire are, for the most part, bursting at the seams with patients and health professionals, focussing on medical imperatives. If I want a job, I will go to the Job Centre. If I want a jab, I will go to the Jab Centre. I remain to be convinced of the benefits of integrating these two disciplines.

***

On the Beat

September 2005

Seven years ago, when I was Shadow Secretary of State for Defence, I enrolled into the Armed Forces Parliamentary Scheme, spending some 30 days as a soldier. And a valuable insight into life in the Armed Forces it gave me, as I spent time in the trenches with the heroes and heroines who compose today's Army; and I spent time too on the Parade Ground with those who had recently enrolled. MPs were treated just like the rest – it is a long time since I was called a tosser. But the scheme enabled me to speak on defence-related matters with added credibility and commitment.

With Law and Order going up the political agenda, and much argument about how the country should be policed, I have now subscribed to a sister project – the Police Parliamentary Scheme. I am grateful to Hampshire's Chief Constable, Paul Kernaghan, and to

Inspector Laurie Rickwood for putting together an instructive programme, embracing Cowes Week, a Southampton FC home game, and, less glamorously, a substantial amount of time on the beat, in Inner City Southampton.

My conclusions must await the completion of the scheme, which I am about halfway through. But the programme has already had its moments of drama. I spent a morning at the Firearms Unit at Netley, where Police Officers are trained to carry firearms. They are confronted with a number of challenging scenarios and their reactions to them are carefully monitored. I was handed a rifle which was wired up to a computer, and asked to watch a video.

My mission was to rescue a child who had been kidnapped by a villain who had taken the child to a shopping centre. I was told that he had a gun in his belt and given a description of his clothes. My instructions were to aim the rifle at the suspect; and squeeze the trigger if and when the appropriate moment presented itself. The video started and it all happened very quickly.

I was shot no less than three times by the kidnapper before I fired back, hitting, as the computer tactlessly revealed, some cereals in a passer-by's trolley. Shoot too soon, and there is an inquiry and a possible prison sentence. Shoot too late and you're dead. I left, full of admiration for those who go on the course, pass it and then have to handle these critical incidents.

I have also been on the beat in the small hours of the morning with the Licensing Unit in Southampton. We called on a large number of nightclubs, checked that the CCTV's were working, and that the bouncers were accredited and had signed the register. We went into one popular nightclub where there was a large hen party. Seeing the two uniformed and helmeted officers come in, a cheer went up. "Hoorah, the strippers have arrived…"

***

Travelling Circus

January 2005

As those MPs who are not planning to stand again announce their retirement, I recall the process of transition in North West Hants, when my predecessor Sir David Mitchell said in 1995 he was standing down as the local MP. The selection process was activated, and I recall being asked, in the final round, whether, if chosen, I would move to the constituency. "Of course" I replied. I glanced at my wife, and noticed she had turned white. I triumphed and, in the interval between my adoption in November that year and the General Election in 1997, no one could have been kinder than Sir David in introducing me to the electorate.

We toured every branch of our great Party, at which Sir David would introduce me with the same joke. No one heard it twice, apart from me and the agent. And we heard it about 60 times. As the weeks grew by, I became fond of it and each time Sir David told his story, I would retaliate with an identical one of my own. We toured the constituency with our duet.

To commemorate this exchange and the smooth transition, I commissioned David Butler to encapsulate in a cartoon the two stories, against a North West Hampshire background. It is below; but it is possible that it might not be understood without the relevant narratives.

Sir David. "The Parochial Church Council was having difficulty choosing a new Vicar. The candidates were too high, or too low; too young or too old. Eventually the Bishop showed some impatience and came to a meeting of the Parochial Church Council. He opened the meeting with a prayer. "O Lord, please bestow upon this parish the succour it so clearly deserves." At which point, Sir David would wave towards me "And this is the sucker you so clearly deserve." There was then laughter and applause.

This would be my cue to respond.

Sir George. "Sir David's amusing and original story reminds me of the Victorian circus proprietor, whose star performer was the human cannonball. People travelled miles to witness him being propelled hundreds of yards through the air. One day, sadly, the man with the gunpowder misjudged the quantity required, and the human cannonball was propelled to eternity. Told of the tragedy, the proprietor commented "How sad; we will never find another man of the same calibre."

At which point, I would bow, with reverence to Sir David, and repeat the proprietor's words.

Scam

June 2005

Where would you find the largest collection of widows with hundreds of millions of pounds in the bank? This may be a question which impoverished bachelors in North West Hampshire ask themselves. Florida? Monte Carlo? Saudi Arabia?

Having analysed my emails, I can give the answer; Lagos. Readers may have heard from these ladies, who have so much in common – and so much that is tragic. For they were all apparently married to the country's Minister for Oil; this public-spirited individual found his career sadly and prematurely terminated, when he was executed by the country's unscrupulous military dictator. But, before his demise, he had taken it upon himself to place a large amount of the revenues for which he was responsible beyond the reach of his persecutor. A precaution for which the nation would doubtless be grateful.

These funds lie safe but dormant in a bank account, access to which can only be secured through the good offices of the grieving widow.

Unfortunately – perhaps because he was busy marrying so many ladies or because of the imminence of the threat to his life - the extraction of the money from this account, so it might be restored to the Nigerian taxpayer, is less than straightforward.

And this is where I - or to be more accurate, sirgeorgeyoung@btinternet.com - come in, along with several hundred other readers of this column. We have been fortunate enough to have been selected by the grieving widow to assist in this patriotic task. News of our shining integrity had reached her ears and, with apologies for approaching us without a formal introduction, she now throws herself at our feet. The funds in question need to be legitimised through our bank account; and, for a commission running into millions of dollars, we are asked to assist by informing her of its details.

Readers are advised to leave the good lady to mourn in peace. But there is a more worrying scam to which people are falling prey. Too many of my constituents have found themselves confronted with a large telephone bill because, unbeknownst to them, their computer has been infected with a rogue dialler, that has been busy dialling premium rate numbers. Others have had a text message, inviting them to dial a premium rate number with a long pre-recorded message, to claim a non-existent cash prize.

I am on the case; I have had meetings with ICSTIS – the custodian of premium rate numbers – and with BT, the organisation through which the rip-off merchants are paid.

The position is complex but essentially unsatisfactory. Although it is clear within a few days that a fraud is under way, it is often months before anything happens. And then a fine is levied on the offending organisation which because, surprise surprise, it is based outside the UK, is never paid. Indeed, our grieving widow in Lagos may be consoling herself by diversifying into this related racket.

***

The Bus

July 2005

On March 2nd, I got a letter from Hampshire County Council. "We are writing to advise you of new Department of Transport legislation that affects our Cango bus services. The new legislation means that all journeys now must be booked, unless you are travelling from a timed stop to another timed stop."

I pottered down to the bus shelter in the village to check its status. It had no green flag – so it was not a timed stop. Inside, a warning notice had been pinned up to warn the putative bus passenger "New legislation requires the passenger travelling on Cango to book their journeys."

But why should I have to book my place, if the bus was going through the village anyway? What had happened to John Prescott's campaign to get us out of our cars?

I wrote to my successor but three at the Department of Transport to ask why he was placing additional hurdles in the path of the nation's bus passengers. My protest was swept aside in the reply "The new regulations that came into force on Feb 23rd offer an unparalleled degree of flexibility to allow operators to run bus services that are completely demand-responsive." This sat uneasily with the Hampshire letter, placing a different interpretation on what had happened.

The Minister then shot himself in the foot, with a sentence his spin-doctor had failed to erase. "I agree that the booking requirement is an inflexibility."

You can say that again. My bus journey is at 7.48 on a Monday morning, from Penton Mewsey to Andover Railway station. But I don't know for certain that I will be on it every week. And, when I have finalised my plans over the weekend, the booking office is closed.

The reason the Minister gave for this inflexibility is so obscure it deserves quotation in full. "Without this provision, a taxi operator could surrender their taxi licence, obtain a bus operator's licence and continue to provide a taxi service under the guise of a flexible bus, eg a vehicle operating from a stop outside an airport or railway station taking passengers to any destination they specify. I should clarify that any such arrangements would not only be in breach of the primary legislation on registering bus services, but also seriously undermine both the taxi and bus licensing systems, making enforcement of both regimes extremely difficult." From these portentous, if obscure arguments, flowed the requirement for villagers in Penton to prebook their place on the bus that had hitherto stopped, like any other bus, if someone was at the bus-stop.

I persisted, and opened up a fresh front with Hampshire County Council. They replied on May 10th "One of our officers has visited the office of the Traffic Commissioner in Bristol and has negotiated a more flexible approach to the new flexible routing legislation. To enable you to use the Cango services to get to the railway station, we will reinstate Penton Mewsey as a timed stop on the C1 service which will mean you do not have to pre-book the journey."

Just as well. My wife, who provides the only other means of getting me to the station, had followed the Department's line of argument closely and decided she too would only get up and take me if I pre-booked.

***

Switch Off

August 2005

Over the Summer Recess, I have been listening to the radio and watching TV more often than usual. Most of the time, it is enjoyable and informative, but there are a number of occasions when I have turned the set on, to be greeted with remarks that have me instantly reaching for the off button. Readers will have their own trigger phrases at which they zap; here are a selection of mine.

"..comes to the rostrum to conduct the first broadcast performance in this country of…"
"..but if you think Nadia should be the next Housemate to be evicted, dial 090 7…"
"…Scottish League First Division, Brechin City Nil…"
"Melissa has £630,000 from selling her pied-a-terre in Notting Hill to find a small flat in Lewisham and a rural retreat near Swaffham..."
"..will explain how to download a new ring-tone for your mobile.."
"…for those of you who have asked some friends round for a barbecue tomorrow, you may not want to hear the weather forecast for Bank Holiday Monday…."

"...as the Fifth Test has been interrupted by rain, our Test Match Special commentators will describe the cakes they have been sent by some of the kind listeners..."

"..Book at Bedtime this week features the recently published book, "The Seafood Diet of the 17th Century Australian Aborigine.."

"...ring Maureen on 118 212, 118 212, 118 212..."

"..if you have been involved in an accident which is no fault of your own, please call Personal Injury Solicitors on...

"..if you agree with this campaign, please write to your local Member of Parliament at the House of Commons, London SW1A..."

"..we now go over to the Olympic pool for the preliminary rounds of the synchronised swimming..."

"...we have Amanda on the line, who wants to give listeners some intimate details of the affair she had fifteen years ago in a Barbados hotel with an English football coach..."

"...we go now to a spokesman from the Health and Safety Executive, who will explain the risks you face if you let your neighbour's children climb the trees in your back garden...."

"do you want to know who is responsible for your council tax going up? We ask the Local Government Minister, a representative from the Local Government Association and Prof Tony Travers of the LSE to explain the intricacies of the latest Revenue Support Grant settlement..."

Happy listening and viewing.

Rubbish

August 2005

As a former civil servant, I was sorry that so many of my former colleagues took industrial action recently. My only direct intervention in a strike was some thirty years ago. The refuse collectors in Lambeth, where Aurelia and I were councillors, went on strike because the council was planning to get rid of totting. (Younger readers may not know about totting; the dustmen used to go through one's bin and, if they found anything of value, they would remove it and put it on a trailer behind the dustcart. Or, if it was an indiscreet photograph, sell it to Private Eye.) They would then go to the totter – in council time - and keep any proceeds of sale. Every local authority had got rid of this unhygienic activity, which both opened up and slowed down the collection process; but the Lambeth dustmen were deeply attached to this perk. When we decided to get rid of it, they went on strike. The councillors collected the rubbish in hired lorries at the weekends. It was an eye-opening, nay eye-smarting, experience that taught me a lot about my neighbours' way of life.

It came as a surprise to me to be offered ten pound notes by local shopkeepers for collecting their rubbish. "It's paid for in your rates" I explained. "But we always give the dustmen £10" came the reply.

After a few weeks, the dustmen returned to work on the terms originally offered and totting was ended. Today, with renewed emphasis on the recycling of rubbish, there may well be attempts to bring back totting, in which case I dare say the dustmen will go on strike again.

During the strike, some people were at a loss to know how to dispose of their rubbish. One ingenious resident put it in a huge cardboard box, wrapped it with expensive paper and a ribbon and left it on the rear seat of his unlocked car. Overnight, it vanished.

**

The CSA

August 2005

Readers will have seen reports of the difficulties in which the Child Support Agency now finds itself, culminating in the resignation of its Chief Executive. Members of Parliament are all too familiar with the work of the CSA; not because we have abandoned our wives and families in droves and then failed to support them; but because, for many of us, it is the largest single generator of work at our Advice Bureaux.

When the state interposes itself into a broken relationship, it risks attracting to itself the bitterness previously focussed on the ex-partner. And if the state is less than efficient in discharging its responsibilities, folk will come to see their MP who, for them, is the local manifestation of that remote entity. We can explain the purpose of the legislation – that parents should support their children if they are in a position so to do, rather than the taxpayer. Taking sides is difficult; who is right in the following true case taken from my records?

An irate ex-wife came to see me, asserting that her ex-husband had lied about his income to the CSA, thereby reducing his payments to her on behalf of their children. He was a self-employed builder and, before they split up, she used to do his books. She knew all too well what he really earned and this was a figure substantially higher than that which he declared first to the Inland Revenue, and subsequently to the CSA. Further, when he had recently returned the children from his access weekend, he had done so in a new Mercedes, whereas she had but a bicycle. And he had just built a conservatory for a local hedge-fund manager. Would I please put the CSA investigators on to him, so his true income could be assessed and justice could be done?

I wrote a suitable letter to the CSA and a man presented himself at my Advice Bureau two weeks later, covered in a light layer of plaster and in ill-humour.

His ex-wife, to whom he had given the marital home worth half a million pounds when she started an affair with another man, was making life difficult. The children in question were all at school, his ex-wife was a qualified accountant, and she should get off her fat butt and get a job. The wealthy boyfriend who had cuckolded the builder of conservatories had moved in with her, but she continued to claim Income Support. The DWP were unaware of her cohabitation as she had failed to declare her change of circumstances. He, the ex-husband, in the meantime, had remarried and had acquired four stepchildren that he was now supporting. Some idiot had now put the CSA fraud squad on to him, when they should be chasing his ex-wife.

I smiled sympathetically.

Useless prize

September 2005

I quite often win a raffle prize. This is a function of the number of raffle tickets I buy – large - and the odds of each one winning a prize – smaller. When I empty my pockets at the weekend, there are enough tickets to supply a cloakroom for a fortnight; except, of course, the counterfoils are scattered across North West Hampshire. And, in the kitchen at home, there are the products of the tickets - bottles.

Prizes in North West Hampshire tend to be bottle-shaped; indeed, I have won the same bottle more than once and some do the rounds. "Aha - the Francois d'Aubigne Vin Mousseux Brut; and matured for another year. We must be in Baughurst."

Last week, I won a prize that was not bottle-shaped. It was an electric ice scraper.

At the moment, when the car's windscreen is obscured by ice, I fill the kettle up with warm water and sprinkle it over the windscreen and windows. The whole operation is manual, and takes about a minute. I assumed the electric ice scraper would save time. But then I read the instructions, reproduced below in inverted commas.

1.   "Before using and after each use, wipe the unit clean with a soft cloth to remove any particles of dirt on element or casing." Note the wording; it is not enough to have wiped it after the last occasion it was used; before using and after use. So, before I can use it in the morning, it has to be groomed.

Then

2.   "To prevent the car battery from being exhausted, keep the engine running when the scraper is in use." This means that, before the windscreen can be defrosted, I have to get into the car – not just to plug the ice scraper into the cigarette lighter; but also to fire the engine up, with the consequent CO_2 emissions.

We then progress to

3. "Please allow the unit to become hot before attempting to melt snow or ice."

This means that, while the unit gets hot, its owner gets cold, sitting in a freezing car, waiting for the unit to acquire sufficient heat to enable it to discharge its function.

And then we have

4. "The metal heater SHOULD NEVER come into direct contact with the glass."

This means painstaking application – using the skills of a barber with a cut-throat razor – so the heater touches the wafer thin layer of ice, but not the glass underneath. Not the work of a moment on six large panes of glass with a shivering hand.

We than graduate to

5. "Allow the product to cool thoroughly before storing." So you can't put it away in its box until it is cool; and of course you have to do the other half of 1.

Someone else may be the fortunate winner of an unused electric ice-scraper at the next charity event I attend.

***

Bronco

September 2005

And so, while the rest of the world watched Live 8, to Monxton for the Village Hoe-Down, to help raise funds for Monxton Village Hall and Amport School. A splendid event with a capacity crowd of 200, superbly organised by local enthusiasts.

The star attraction was a Bucking Bronco, a mechanical replica of the screen version we have all seen at the rodeos of America. This simulated the movements of a progressively enraged bull, while the rider saw how long he (or she – well done, Rhonda) could remain mounted. An electronic stopwatch at the ringside measured the tenacity of the rider, with the winner securing a percentage of the combined entry fees of 50p each.

Early on in the evening, a number of constituents politely inquired about my availability for this spectator sport. I had devised the perfect alibi. I would mount the monster to raise funds if the Vicar, who was also present, would do the same. I had established from the Vicar's wife that they were going on a walking holiday in the Lake District on the Monday, and her consent for this high-risk adventure would be withheld.

So, imagine my alarm when, an hour later, I saw the Vicar remove his spectacles, stride into the ring and leap into the saddle, to a chorus of cheers from his parishioners. Once in place, the popular priest mouthed a silent prayer, crossed himself and contemplated martyrdom. The operator flicked the switch and, with an irreverent shrug of its shoulders, the bull sent the gentleman of the cloth flying through the air to rejoin his congregation. The ringside clock barely moved.

The local MP, inconveniently reminded of his pledge, was then summoned. One of those present, a prominent political opponent, was hoping that the bull might do what the electorate had failed to do a few weeks earlier, namely unseat the incumbent.

Alas, I fared little better than the Vicar, though I looked the part as I had brought with me some appropriate headgear. I was in the saddle for as long as it takes the Speaker to shout "Order, Order."

The representatives of two of the Estates of the Realm consoled each other that their respective qualities lay elsewhere, as their wives escorted them away from any further temptations. As I left, I heard a cry from my political opponent. "What a tosser!" He means the bull, I assured my wife.

***

The Shark

November 2005

Planning is in the news again. At one end of the constituency, proposals to develop land at Manydown before 2011 are given the thumbs down by the Inspectors; at the other end, Picket Twenty looks like remaining semi-detached from Andover. There will be some sighs of relief by those who opposed these developments, but many will hold their breath until the local councils have responded and the process is complete. Where will Prescott the Predator strike next?

I confess to having left my mark on the landscape. Some time ago, as Planning Minister, an appeal from a shark crossed my desk. This shark was not a property developer, but a life-size replica of Carcharodon Carcharias.

To be precise, the owner of a plastic Great White Shark had inserted it, incisors first, through his roof. He had inflicted this indignity on the beast without taking the precaution of applying for planning permission from Oxford City Council. (Inserting a shark into your home constitutes "development" under the Town and Country Planning Act 1990.)

When this oversight was brought to their attention, the civic leaders of that great City served an enforcement notice on the shark's owner, requiring him to extricate it and restore the integrity of the suburban skyline. The owner applied for retrospective consent, which was declined. He appealed and an Inspector was appointed to adjudicate as to whether half a shark should continue to reside in the attic – (or, more accurately, whether the other half should continue to live outside it.)

The Inspector's findings landed on my desk, with advice from my officials. The appeal should be disallowed was their clear recommendation. Otherwise, the country's skyline would be dominated by millions of waving dorsal fins and tails as this new ruling was exploited. The very integrity of the planning system would be challenged.

I demurred. While I didn't want to be surrounded by inverted plastic fish at rooftop level, I did want to live in a country where some eccentric can put half a shark in his attic without being steamrollered by an insensitive bureaucracy. But we needed to find a reason for allowing the appeal. We discovered that the Oxford District Plan had a policy of decentralising tourism from the centre to the fringe of the City. The Headington shark had become a curiosity for visitors, and was on the outskirts. Hey presto, the shark was in conformity with the plan.

So the appeal was allowed; to this day, the shark remains accommodated in the upper storey of a terraced house in Headington. While I would not put myself in the same class as Sir Christopher Wren, I hope someone may say of me one day "Si monumentum requiris, circumspice."

***

Smoking

Jan 2006

For the past few weeks when Parliament has been sitting, I have spent Tuesday and Thursday, morning and afternoon, on a Standing Committee, examining line by line the Government's legislative ambitions for the NHS. We have debated the clinical skills of the pharmacist, and the ophthalmologist; but I am afraid we spent most of our time in the pub. Metaphorically.

The most controversial section of the Bill was the Government's proposal to divide the pubs in England into two – those that sold food and those that did not. The former would have to ban smoking; and the second would not.

I am, unashamedly, on the health side of the argument as opposed to the tobacco side. When I was a Health Minister, I tried to get the health warning not just on the cigarette packs, but on the cigarettes themselves. The manufacturers resisted, arguing that the ink, when burnt and inhaled, might damage the smoker's health. I jest not.

In the Standing Committee, opponents of the Government's policy developed the argument that to distinguish between pubs that sold food and pubs that didn't was illogical, from the point of view of the bar staff – whose health was one of the Government's concerns. We had a serious discussion as to when a bag of crisps became so big that it was no longer a snack (allowable in a smoking pub) and became food (not-allowable). We discovered that the publican could not provide the apples that came from the tree in his garden to his customers, without becoming a pub that sold food. (But he could provide less healthy salted nuts and still allow smoking.)

Throughout this debate, confronted with powerful arguments shredding the Government's policy, the Minister stuck to her (smoking) guns. I have no idea whether she believed what she said or not, but she did a heroic job defending the distinction.

One MP put the time of this debate to the productive task of signing Christmas cards - a process that continued, worryingly, right up to the last day we sat before Christmas, Tuesday December 20th

At the end of the debate, we forced a vote on this absurd distinction; the Government scraped home by one. They were saved by the vote of a Scottish MP to whose constituents the law would not apply – the matter having been devolved to Holyrood. Indeed, his constituents have the benefit of a wholly smoke-free environment, whether the pub sells apples or not. I had no influence over that devolved decision, but thanks to the topsy-turvy world in which we now live, a Scottish MP can decide what happens in the White Hart, Penton Mewsey. I cannot influence what happens in the Thistle and Sporran – an uncomfortable combination – in Falkirk.

No sooner had the Bill completed its passage through Standing Committee than the Government announced there would be a free vote on this issue at the Report Stage. The Secretary of State for Health promptly declared that, unshackled from collective responsibility, she would be supporting the line I had advocated in Committee. All pubs are now smoke free.

And people wonder why nobody trusts Ministers.

A Night at the Ballet

Feb 2006

When the bells go off in the House of Commons, it means one of four things. The House has begun its session; the House has ended its session; there is a division. Or there is a fire.

Thus the bells usually ring at 2.30 and at 10.30 to mark the kick-off and the close of play. And they go off intermittently in between, when the Nation's elected representatives are unable to agree on whatever proposition is in front of them.

Like Pavlovian dogs, we are conditioned. When the bells ring at 2.30, we head for the Chamber; when they ring at 10.30 – for the adjournment - we head for home. And if they ring in between, we head for the Division Lobbies, where a well-informed and courteous Whip gives guidance as to whether we are in favour of or against the proposition that has provoked dissent.

So, when the bells went at 4.15pm last Wednesday, I headed for the Lobbies. But I had been sold a dummy. The debate on the Merchant Shipping Bill had ended early and without dissent, and that was the Going Home Bell.

We know from the press that MPs find all sorts of ways of amusing themselves when they are alone in London. And I succumbed to temptation.

I rang up the Royal Opera House, Covent Garden and booked a ticket for Giselle. Or, as it turned out, for Gise...

Let me explain. My ticket was numbered AA30. In financial circles, a double or triple A rating is good news, indicating status and prosperity. In musical circles, they work on the opposite principle.

Seats in Row AA are not for those who suffer from vertigo. They are at the highest point of the building, where the atmosphere becomes rare. My fellow buffs and I were provided not with a fire exit, but with oxygen masks and parachutes.

Not only were we very high; but we were at one extremity of the building, privileged to enjoy what the Opera House describes as a

Restricted View. Only part of the stage was visible, so it was with some relief that the only prop on the stage, when the curtain rose, was on that part that I could see. It was a bench.

The relief did not last long. Giselle is a ballet; and, if there is an object on the stage, that is the part of the stage you don't dance on.

And, so, instead of seeing Giselle, I saw Gise... I admired the prima bal...ina, performing some athletic entrech..s and working well with the cor.s de bal..t in their tut.s; The choreo.....phy was fantastic.

But I cannot complain; the ticket only cost £7. Next time the business collapses, I will pay £7 for ticket ZZ30, and see ..selle.

***

The Whips

April 2006

I was having a cup of coffee in the Members' Tea Room on a Thursday, when a Whip approached me.

"We are looking for a high quality contribution from a former Treasury Minister in the Budget debate today, and I can think of no one better than you, George, to do this. The House always listens to what you have to say."

I used to be a Whip, and I speak their language. What he meant to say was that the rest of the Parliamentary Party were out canvassing for the local elections, and I clearly wasn't. We were short of speakers. If I had nothing better to do than drink coffee, I had better get off my butt and into the Chamber and make a speech. What I decided to say was my problem, not his.

I finished my coffee, picked up the Chancellor's Budget Statement and went to the Chamber to assemble some thoughts. These were shared with a modest audience a few hours later. The Whips are not folk to mess with.

Not a lot of people know about the Whips; their office is a cross between a Social Services Area Office and a branch of Cosa Nostra. They can attend to your needs if you are going through a bad patch; or make life uncomfortable for you if you upset them - in ways that they hint at, but don't usually explain. A Whip who writes a book about The Office is regarded as a traitor, as they are coy about tactics. One gambit that I used to use when I was a Whip was to say "The Leader is thinking of reshuffling the Front Bench, and I know he/she would be impressed if (or disappointed if)..." depending on the behaviour one was trying to influence. No commitment was ever made.

I was in the Whips Office at a time when the House still sat through the night and Jim Callaghan had a precarious majority. One night, I contacted my flock to warn them that their presence would be required until the session ended, and this would be around breakfast time.

One MP came back to me with a heart-rending story; it was his 25th Wedding Anniversary that day. He and his wife had been planning an elaborate evening together and this unexpected change in Parliamentary business threatened this celebration. My heart melted; I let him off, on condition that, if we really needed him in the small hours of the morning, he would come back when summoned.

As the night wore on, the Government's majority got smaller and smaller, as the elderly Labour MPs defied their Whips and went home. At 2am, I rang my colleague to summon him to the House. His wife answered the phone. No, he wasn't there and she hadn't seen him all day; he had told her he would be at the House for an all-night sitting.

Wild horses won't drag his name from me. Omerta.

Keep my Seat

June 2006

Railway privatisation was not the most popular policy that I have put on the statute book; but it does have one advantage. At the moment, a number of transport companies, including the incumbent Stagecoach, are bidding for the franchise for South West Trains which is up for renegotiation. Under British Rail, there was never this opportunity to test the market, drive a better bargain for travellers and taxpayers, and inject some competition into what was an unchallenged and at times cosy monopoly.

The outcome may be a better performing service; but my recent problem with the trains was not with the operator, but with a passenger.

The 5.20 from Waterloo to Basingstoke and Andover is a popular train, taking wealth creators back to their homes and families in Hampshire after a tough day in the Smoke. So popular is it that sometimes there is nowhere to sit.

Catching it recently, I arrived ten minutes before departure and sat down. Shortly afterwards, a lady came down the aisle and placed an expensive woman's magazine on the table next to me. "Would you please keep this place for me?" she asked, in a tone to which the only acceptable answer was "Yes". Keeping seats is what we members of the House of Commons are used to, but usually for ourselves.

She then vanished off the train in a cloud of scent, confronting me with a moral dilemma. For, within seconds, other passengers – many of them constituents - sought to place themselves in the seat reserved for the Reader of the Magazine. Harassed elderly ladies, perspiring gently in the heat, made a beeline for what eventually became the only unoccupied seat in the carriage, and began manoeuvring themselves into place.

"I am afraid someone is sitting there" I said. "I don't see anybody" was the usual response, followed by a look of hatred. For five minutes, I fought a stout rearguard action on behalf of the Vanishing

Lady who, for all I knew, was busy buying yet more expensive magazines and scent on the station concourse and might miss the train. What was worse – to let someone take the seat and risk a public denunciation for lack of chivalry when she returned? Or to become yet more unpopular with my regular travelling companions?

With seconds to spare, she returned, sat in the seat for which I had almost given if not my life at least a useful chunk of my parliamentary majority. She proffered a perfunctory nod of appreciation in my direction, unaware of the dramas that had taken place in her absence.

Dear Lady, if you are somewhere out there – please don't ask me to do that again. Whatever it is you want to buy – I'll buy it. And you can keep my seat while I do so.

***

Little People come to Stay

July 2006

We are always pleased to have the grandchildren to stay, although it is nice to get one's life back again when they depart. The focal point of their visit is the Penton Mewsey Tennis Course, organised by the heroic and patient Diana Kruger. This keeps the little ones exercised, but only for a portion of the time when they are awake. For the rest of the time, heroism and patience has to be displayed closer to home. I give warning to Finkley Farm and the Hawk Conservancy that trouble will be heading their way.

For the benefit of fellow grandparents confronted with a similar challenge, here are the answers to the questions that will be put to us.

"Because there is a little sign on the cover which says that DVD is not suitable for children."

"When you are 18."

"Because the cutters inside the shredder will turn your fingers into little strips, like those pieces of paper at the bottom of the bin. And the Minor Injury Unit at Andover Hospital is closed."

"Because your grandmother wants to watch Three Men in a Boat."

"Because it might rain."

"Because it will make you sick."

"Because that is very expensive paper with a green crest on it your grandfather uses to write to people on.. No, I am sure he has never described them as boring, or time wasters, or mad. You can draw on the back of his Select Committee Report."

"Because it is now half past eleven and it is my bedtime."

"Because you broke it last time you were here."

"Because those aren't sweets, they are your grandmother's headache pills. No – only when you come to stay."

"Because it won't work if you put marmalade on the keyboard."

"Because they are not ripe yet."

"Because that is for the birds to eat."

"No. The attic is out of bounds."

"That's the smoke alarm. It goes off when you play around with the switch on the toaster."

"Because His Worshipful the Mayor hasn't asked you to his party."

"Because your grandfather hasn't read it yet."

"I don't care if your father does let you do that at your home. You are not doing it here."

"That is horse manure…. because it is still hot - No you can't warm Barbie's hands in it…"

"Because I say not."

"Because that turns on the underfloor heating. "

"No, not in August."

"Because if you touch that switch, I won't be able to finish what I am writ…."

***

Horn Concerto

September 2006

I wrote an article a few weeks ago about a family holiday in the South West; there is a risk that another column about a holiday will reinforce the impression that MPs spend the whole of the summer recess by the seaside. I confess to having spent two weeks away from the constituency; but all the time I was linked to North West Hampshire by a virtual umbilical cord. Thanks to modern technology, I could keep the Child Support Agency and Her Majesty's Customs and Excise, the two major generators of complaints from constituents, on their toes from an internet café in Zagreb, with a glass of cold Karlovacko at hand.

We have just returned from a week in Croatia, seeking raw material for a talk Aurelia is giving about her father who was born there. After a day in Town Halls, Museums and Cemeteries, we looked for culture and relaxation. One evening, we went to a superb concert given by the Zagreb Philharmonic Orchestra. One of the works that was performed was the Richard Strauss Horn Concerto.

As a former wind-player myself, I know the difficulty of playing this instrument. The principal ingredient of that which is blown into the mouthpiece is compressed air; but an associated ingredient is water. If the quality of output from the horn is not to be degraded and sound like a gargle, water has to be released from the instrument at regular intervals.

There is no way of doing this elegantly. After the opening salvo in this concerto, the composer leaves a gap of enough bars for the soloist to attend to the needs of his instrument. The soloist removed the mouthpiece, turned the instrument upside down, and then committed a minor act of indecency in a public place. We pretended to look the other way; but there was more to come.

Later on in the first movement, the soloist removed a section of the horn's colon to attend to some intestinal distress, performed some First Aid with his little finger; and re-assembled the instrument in time for the next blast.

What happened next, we will never know. For when the time came for the horn's next comfort break, the soloist turned his back on the audience. What took place was a secret between him and the first viola player, whose gaze was averted by being focussed on the score. But we were concerned about the puddle at the soloist's foot, as if a puppy had relieved itself. Would the conductor slip on it? Should horn players carry a sponge in their pockets?...

The Pumpkin

October 2006

As I write this column, I hear on the radio that the police are going to crack down on anti-social behaviour connected with Halloween. I plead guilty to a relevant offence.

Over the past few weeks, Aurelia and I have attended many a Harvest Supper and joined in seasonal hymns before sitting down. We have Ploughed the Fields and Scattered all over North West Hampshire, and then dined handsomely on the produce of the soil. Quarley, Appleshaw and Wolverton have hosted memorable feasts.

After the Quarley Harvest Supper, there was an auction for local produce, raising funds to help replace the stolen church bells. I found myself, under moral pressure from the Churchwarden on my left, to bid for one of the largest pumpkins I had ever seen. The Body Mass Index was off the scale and, for £15 it was mine. Two people were required to carry it to the car.

What does one do with a pumpkin the size of Les Dawson?

Then we remembered. Our five year old grand-daughter was growing a pumpkin from seed in time for Halloween. The last time we saw it, it was the size of a small tomato. One night we visited her home, with the pumpkin in the back of the car. The umbilical cord securing the tomato-sized pumpkin to its mother was severed, and Les Dawson was put in its place. We left him with his new foster-mother.

The effect on the grand-daughter the following morning was reported to be dramatic. She was on the cusp of abandoning her belief in fairies, and joining her two older brothers in a more adult understanding of the world she lives in. This incident has delayed the progression for a month or two.

And if the police in Berkshire are looking for the perpetrators of an anti-social Halloween related crime, it's a fair cop. But we got rid of the pumpkin.

***

Ministerial Code

November 2006

Earlier this month, I spoke in a debate in the House of Commons. We were discussing whether MPs should receive an additional allowance – a Communication Allowance – of £10,000. This was to enable us to bridge the democratic gulf that has opened up between elected and elector. I am favour of communicating with my constituents and recognise that I should do more and do it better; but I am against spending a penny more of your hard earned taxes than is necessary. I therefore spoke and voted against this new allowance. (I lost.)

Through the hospitality of the Andover Advertiser, I am able to communicate with many on a fortnightly basis for nothing (though the reader has to pay 55p). But I can now reveal, exclusively, how even this important exercise in democratic dialogue can be threatened.

As the MP for Ealing Acton, with a majority one tenth that of the current one, my column in the Ealing Gazette was a electoral lifeline. When the Conservative Party and I were accused on a regular basis of taking a hatchet to popular public services, the column was a weekly testament to my gentle humanity. However, when I rejoined the Government after a period in exile, I got a letter from the Cabinet Secretary, drawing my attention to Para 105 of Questions of Procedure for Ministers. This important limb of the British Constitution may be unknown to readers, so I reproduce it below.

"Any Minister wishing to practice regular journalism, including the contribution of weekly or fortnightly articles to local newspapers in their constituencies, must have the prior approval of the Prime Minister. In cases of doubt, and in all cases where a Minister is contemplating the contribution of an article going beyond the strict confines of his or her Departmental responsibility, the Prime Minister should be consulted, before work has begun and in any case before any commitment to publish is entered into. In all cases where an article contains material which falls within the Departmental responsibility of another Minister, that Minister must be consulted."

As Secretary of State for Transport, my constituents had a limited appetite for my views on road pricing, motorway widening, bus deregulation and Terminal 5. My articles had been up until then wide-ranging. But if they were to continue, John Major, who as Prime Minister had many other things on his mind at the time, would have had to clear my column in advance. And any comment on any topic other than Transport would have to be cleared or censored by the appropriate Cabinet colleague.

Readers will sympathise with my dilemma. I wanted to maintain the dialogue with my constituents; but I didn't want to break the Ministerial Code. A telephone call to the Editor of the local paper resolved the matter. Would he accept and publish a weekly article entitled "Not the Sir George Young column" in the name of my wife, if I gave him a private assurance that I would continue to be its author? He would.

The arrangement was a triumph. The Prime Minister and the Cabinet Secretary could sleep again at night, knowing that whatever embarrassment would strike the Government, it would not come from the Ealing Gazette. And I was happy that a sympathetic channel of communication had been kept open.

Until one of my constituents came up to my wife and told her "I can't tell you how much the column has improved, since you took it over from George."

***

Got a Light?

January 2007

Many of my constituents have resolved to give up smoking for the New Year, and I wish them well. I renounced the habit when I was at Oxford many years ago, having read the first of many reports by the Royal College of Physicians. I concluded that life was hazardous enough without tilting the odds further towards the Old Man with the Hood and the Scythe (I was driving an Austin Healey 3000 at the time). I stubbed out my last Gold Leaf forty years ago and my index finger slowly returned to a normal colour.

Those who follow my contributions in the House of Commons will know that I am a member of the provisional wing of the anti-smoking brigade when it comes to legislating against tobacco. It was rumoured that Margaret Thatcher moved me from my post as a Health Minister because of my aggressive negotiating posture with the tobacco companies. They resisted my perfectly reasonable suggestion that the health warning should be, not just on every packet, but on every cigarette. I am delighted that, as from this summer, smoking will be banned in all public places - including the less-than-public Smoking Room in the House of Commons, (which will nonetheless continue to be known as the Smoking Room.)

However, my reputation for Puritanism nearly came unstuck. As a Junior Minister in the 1979 Parliament, my job was to answer my Department's Adjournment Debates at the end of the day's proceedings in the House. One day, I was scheduled to reply to a debate on Health Education.

I had sent my driver home, and, in the spirit of the debate I was about to contribute to, I bicycled from my Department to the House of Commons.

During that short journey, the heavens opened. A month's rainfall fell in five minutes, and all on my shoulders. I got absolutely drenched and arrived at the Members' Entrance five minutes before the debate was due to start, looking like Dustin Hoffman in the Graduate, but without the headgear.

I dashed into one of the bars, and found a journalist who was nearly my size. I asked him if I could borrow his jacket so it might adorn the Government benches in the Chamber. He readily obliged – sensing a diary story in the making - but first removing his wallet. (He was from the Glasgow Herald.)

The jacket was nearly the same colour as my trousers, and, if I stood close up against the despatch box, hopefully no one would notice any disparity of material.

After a short debate, I replied, hoping no one would spot the growing pool of water at my feet.

Towards the end of my speech, I needed to wipe my brow; not from perspiration, but from the rain which was filtering through my hair. I fumbled in the jacket pocket, searching for a handkerchief. I found one and pulled it out.

Out it came, along with a packet of 20 king-size, high-tar cigarettes and a box of matches. Mercifully, this was before our proceedings were televised.

Industrial Action

January 2007

To those constituents who had a horrendous journey home on Thursday last week, I have a message. Your Member of Parliament felt your pain. I was at Waterloo Station at 3.30pm, and I got home at 8.30pm.

I boarded a train that the departure board said was going to Basingstoke. This was promising, as there was little else advertised on the board. But when the carriages were crammed full, the sardines were told to disembark.

A group of resourceful passengers found two empty trains; we then found a train driver and guard who were prepared to drive and guard one of them; and a Customer Services Officer who had a hotline to Control. A deal was within our grasp, but foundered on the issue of driver's hours.

One frustrated commuter asked if four others would share a cab to Basingstoke. There were four volunteers, one of whom was your MP.

We had first to find a black cab prepared to do the journey. "Basingstoke? Is that out Barking way?" When we told him where it was, he declined. We found one who had a full tank, an empty bladder, a flask of coffee, Sat Nav and a wife who didn't mind if he never came home that night. So off went five total strangers, united only by a desire to get to Basingstoke.

There was Andrew the Jeweller; Sarah the Health Inspector; Sue the Banker; and Sue the Mobile Phone. And me.

Sarah knew a lot about inspecting hospitals; but, working for the NHS, she knew even more about being re-organised. Sue the Mobile Phone worked for Motorola, and had a mobile phone a ten year old would die for. Sue the Banker was in Customer Services and Andrew bought and sold precious stones.

The first hour was spent as the ladies re-arranged their child care. Sarah had five children, all of whom led active social lives. The logistics of managing their movements, horrendous when she was with them, seemed unmanageable in absentia.

Sue the Banker was sitting opposite me and I saw she was looking with horror at my right ear. I was facing backwards, in front of the meter. And it was the meter that was worrying her. While the taxi was stationery for the first hour, its meter was not. And if the banker was worried, we should all be.

Negotiations were opened with the driver for a fixed price contract. The Jeweller was tasked with these negotiations. He spent his life being negotiated down, and had the required portfolio of skills. A bargain was struck at £25 a head.

Sue the Banker had had no lunch, and had been looking forward to an early meal at home. With a long journey ahead – we spent one hour in Victoria Street – we looked round to see whom we would eat first. And decided it would be easier to stop at a Motorway Service Station.

To pass the time, I asked the Jeweller to identify the stones on the many rings being worn by the lady passengers, and then value them. He wasn't going to tiptoe through that minefield. He was not only a jeweller, but a diplomat.

There was a low point during the journey. Sue's husband rang in to say he had caught a train from Waterloo to Basingstoke – and where was she?

But if you had to spend four hours in a confined place with four total strangers, you could not have been more fortunate. All were sober and congenial and, given we were in a very small place, none had personal hygiene problems.

As we disembarked at Basingstoke Station, the taxi driver, who had noted the conviviality in the back of the cab, suggested a reunion in a year's time. We demurred.

European Parliament

February 2007

Britain has been to war with many countries in its glorious military history, and the reasons for some of these conflicts were pretty flimsy. In 1738, for example, Captain Robert Jenkins presented himself before my predecessors in Parliament with his ear; or, to be more accurate, without his ear which, he claimed, had been cut off by the Spanish when they boarded his ship seven years earlier. War was duly declared against Spain in 1739.

One country we have never declared hostilities against is Belgium. But I felt mildly incensed by that otherwise friendly and hospitable country when I went to Brussels last week with my wife.

We were in search of sculptures her father did when he lived in that great city. Pictures were needed of his work to illustrate a talk on his life to be given by Aurelia in the House of Commons next month.

We tracked down his Churchill in the Avenue Winston Churchill; and his Montgomery above Montgomery Metro station. The relevant images were captured on our digital camera.

To complete our mission, we needed to find his Paul Henri Spaak, a former Prime Minister of Belgium and the first President of the European Parliament. We knew his bust was in the lobby of that building, which we found in the shadow of the European Commission.

The building was deserted as our MEPs had migrated to Strasbourg. (Most Parliaments make do with one building but, for some reason, the European Parliament requires two.)

To understand my disappointment at the diplomatic incident which then occurred, the reader needs some background information.

The Mother of Parliaments at Westminster welcomes Members of such upstart democratic institutions as the European Parliament. Not only can they come and go freely, but they are allowed into the very shrine of the building; the Members' Dining Room. They can enjoy wine from our cellars (as long as they pay for it) and contribute to informed political debate as we take refreshment.

I assumed that, when I presented myself to the European Parliament, this hospitality would be reciprocated. I entered a door marked "Centre d'Accréditation" and, in my best French, explained my mission to a lady the other side of the security screen. She was unmoved. "Admission n'est pas possible."

I asked if I might appeal to a higher authority. I was directed towards a man reading a newspaper behind a desk. I produced my House of Commons pass and explained my ambition to take home a digital image of one of his country's finest citizens. No; or, to be exact, Non. Whatever was going to happen to me, I was not going to be accredited.

At that point I saw, some 20 feet away, the very bust I wanted to photograph. I adjusted my negotiation position and outlined a resolution of the impasse. No further trespass need take place on Belgian soil. I just wished to take a photograph from where I was of the founder of European democracy, who was gazing with bemusement at this exchange. The bureaucrat was unmoved. Whatever freedoms were secured by the Treaty of Rome, they did not extend to the free movement of MPs within the European Parliament. We reached an impasse. Despondent, we left the building. Then, from a public place outside, I aimed my camera at the Spaak behind the window.

Frantic gestures from the Centre of Accreditation indicated the illegality of even this action. I ignored them and a picture was taken. (See above.) Fearing arrest and the removal of, if not my ear, then my camera, I gave it to my wife and we headed off in separate directions. If anyone was to be apprehended, it would be me and the images would be secure.

We made it safely back to England without the issue of a European Arrest Warrant; and the talk will take place. I warn those who are coming that the picture of Spaak does him less than justice, and I warn the President of the European Commission that the reasons for this will be made clear.

Slavery

March 2007

With a debate in the House of Commons about Wilberforce and the Abolition of Slavery imminent, it was time to find out what the Youngs were up to during this period of social reform. As those who have researched their ancestors know, this is not a risk-free project; the Youngs could have been on the wrong side.

Mercifully, this turned out not to be the case.

In a speech which he made in the House of Commons on April 18th 1791, William Wilberforce referred to Sir George Young. "An honourable baronet, Sir George Young, and many others, had said they saw the slaves treated in a manner which they were sure their owners would have resented if it had been known to them."

This Sir George was several generations back. While it is relatively easy to trace my ancestors, it is less easy to find out which one is being referred to. This is because, for over 200 years, the eldest son has always been Sir George Young, Bt. This tradition looks set to continue for some time as we have a son called George; and so, by chance, does he.

The one referred to by Wilberforce was serving in the Navy – he went on to become an Admiral – and we have a letter from him dated October 14th 1787. As he contemplated the war clouds over Europe, he wrote "From the present appearance of War, I am induced to request, you will please to acquaint My Lords Commissioners of the Admiralty, that should such an event take place, I should wish to be employed in a more active situation that that of Commander of the Royal Yacht."

In fact, shortly after that he was examined before the bar of the House of Commons on the African Slave Trade and we are told "gave evidence of its evils, not less valuable because temperately worded." This gene of temperate speech has, I hope, passed down the generations

We learn from the Official Report that:

Sir George Young, then a Captain in His Majesty's Navy, gave evidence which was summarised in the Committee's report.

"By the evidence of Sir George Young. He ....observed that they – (the slaves) - "were so crowded, particularly on Board of one ship, that the stench of the hatchway was intolerable." That "the men slaves were chained," while "the women were at liberty."

What struck my ancestor was not just the overcrowding of the slaves; but the poor treatment of the sailors. "They were half starved, ill-cloathed and inhumanly treated by their captains. The reason assigned by the sailors for this ill-treatment was to induce them to run away in the West Indies and forfeit their wages." "A guinea ship seldom returns with more than half her complement and the annual loss of seamen sustained by the nation by the guinea Trade amounts to the manning of two ships of the line."

One has some idea of the problems that confronted Wilberforce when one reads the conclusions of a joint council which reported to Mr Speaker in 1789. "It is notorious our slaves in general are not only treated with kindness and humanity, but they are also protected by law from immoderate chastisement or cruel treatment, and enjoy more easy, comfortable and happy lives, than multitudes of the labourers in Great Britain."

What will my heirs make of my contribution on social reform? Well, they may look up the debate on Lords Reform and find, to their relief, that the sixth baronet spoke and voted for a democratically elected chamber to replace an outdated system of patronage.

BE RIGHT AND PERSIST

Sir George Young, Kn.t

Admiral of the White Squadron.

Satnavs

September 2007

This week we enter what are for me uncharted waters; though in reality they are thoroughfares that have been extensively navigated. My constituency duties have required me to understand the world of satellite navigation.

One of the roads in the constituency has been relegated from the Premier Division to the First Division in the Highway League. The A339 from Newbury to Basingstoke used to be a Road of National Significance and was looked after by the Highways Agency. Following the construction of the Newbury Bypass, it was relegated, and handed over, with no endowment, to Hampshire County Council. Traffic from Oxford to Basingstoke is now meant to go on the A34, A303 and M3, and the route is so signed. It is not meant to go on the A339, and those who live along it are distressed that the volume of traffic has not fallen but risen.

Enter Satellite Navigation, the system that directs Polish lorry drivers through fast-flowing rivers. I summoned one of its players to my office in Westminster. (I am familiar with satnav as the last car I bought arrived with it plumbed in. I get on well with my navigator, a lady from the Home Counties. I believe her to be married with a three year old son, because there is a hint in her enunciation that she is used to speaking to someone with limited intelligence and prone to disobedience.)

I showed Mr Satnav to a chair, saying "You have arrived at your destination. Your route guidance system has been switched off." He smiled weakly. It turned out he was the wrong person to speak to; his company plotted the roads. The company I needed was the next one up in the chain, the one that planned the routes. So I tracked down a big wheel in the dominant company in the business and spoke to him. Let us for the sake of argument call him Mr Tom Thomas.

In the course of our conversation, in which he explained the problems of doing what I wanted him to do, namely re-route traffic along Premier Division roads, he used an adjective to describe the UK road network I have never heard used before.

It was "dynamic". What Mr Thomas meant by "dynamic" was that local authorities sometimes made streets one way; turned them into bus lanes; banned right turns and put up No Entry signs. For the motorist, this is boring and explains why the network is often static. For the Satellite Navigation Industry, it represents dynamism.

Mr Thomas told me it was not possible for satnav to reflect the priorities of the Highways Agency and stop sending people down the A339, until every country in the EU came up with an agreed road hierarchy in a common electronic format. As the European Parliament has been unable to agree for forty years where its Headquarters are, we will have to wait a day or two for Mr Thomas' dream.

But in the course of our conversation, a solution to the A339 problem appeared. Soon, your satnav route will be based on real time information. In other words, it will use actual traffic speeds on the roads in question to direct you to the quickest route to your destination. Were those who live on the A339, for example, to drive extremely slowly along it, depressing average speeds, Mr Tom Thomas would then direct all the traffic elsewhere. You read it here first.

Out to Dinner

October 2007

The considerate hostess at today's dinner party will often brief, in advance, those she has invited to her table. They will be informed about the arrangements for the evening, and about their fellow guests. We were nonetheless surprised to receive the following on a Saturday morning.

"You will find our house in the village without too much difficulty, because there will be a police car outside it. As you may know, William sits as a Recorder, and one of his clients has just come out of prison. The probation officer says he shows no remorse and wants to "put that toff away". The police car is there to deter any unpleasantness. We have given the officer your car number so you are not inconvenienced."

"When you arrive, you will be warmly greeted by Henry, our Irish Wolfhound. He may sound fierce, but he is a real softie. Indeed, you may need to detach him from your leg if he is over-affectionate."

"In addition to William and myself, and of course the two of you, there are four other guests.

David and Cynthia C.

Cynthia has the local "SlimminWimmin" franchise – a weight reduction course for the clinically obese. She will be sitting next to two of the men, but may well try to enrol their wives on the course with her special New Year Resolution Offer "Low Weight in 08." We advise caution; the diet can cause halitosis and the therapy sessions are traumatic.

David is in facilities management. He is a Southampton supporter, and it is worth checking the football results before you come. If the Saints lost, you are advised not to discuss football. His hands may stray under the table between courses (at our last party, this caused the lady on his left to leave early. The lady on his right appeared to enjoy his attention.)

Jacques and Clarissa D.

Clarissa is a clairvoyant. We have used her professionally at Newbury Racecourse and found her unreliable. Her imagination can run away with her and we have asked her not to bring her Ouija Board this time. Her daughter achieved notoriety on Big Brother two years ago and the libel case will be heard next week.

Her husband Jacques is French and, yes, it is a wig. He has just bought the village pub and is turning it into a fish restaurant. This has upset the darts team and the pool players.

He enjoys a glass of wine or two and has a low resistance to alcohol. He may sing the Marseillaise after the sweet. We will provide you with the words so you can join in to save embarrassment.

After dinner and a glass or two of port, we play a game handed down by William's father before he was certified and had to go to Melbury Lodge. We will explain the rules at the time. Bring a small amount of cash. Gentlemen should ensure their belts are not too tight and ladies should not wear necklaces. Let us know if you are on any medication."

*****

Lost Mobile

December 2007

Many constituents have, at some point, mislaid their mobile phone. Often they will turn up again, but occasionally they disappear for ever, having been used to make expensive calls to premium rate lines and then pilfered for whatever raw materials they contain.

Members of Parliament are not immune from this hazard. We try to look after our Blackberries, but they occasionally go astray and you may come across one. They convey messages from the Whips to members of their party and the following will help you to decode the signals they send out.

"There are speaking opportunities on Thursday." This means that the Government have chosen a topic for a debate on which no one wants to speak. This happens from time to time, for example when there is a football match which MPs want to watch. This is a signal from the Whips that they are desperate for speakers.

"The vote scheduled for 8pm will now take place at 9pm." This means that one of our more verbose colleagues has caught Mr Speaker's eye and is on his feet, oblivious of the deal done through the usual channels to end the debate at 8pm.

"The vote scheduled for 10pm has been cancelled." This means that the Government has realised it was likely to lose, has given in to the opposition, conceded the relevant amendment, so no vote is now needed.

"The Sun is doing a survey of MPs. This is likely to be unhelpful and you are advised not to take part." This means that one of the colleagues has confessed to smoking dope at university and another colleague has condemned him. The press are having a field day lining up both sides, and the Whips are trying to cut off the oxygen.

"Please ring the Chief Whip at once." This is probably bad news. This message has not gone out to all the colleagues – only to you. Before you ring him, check today's tabloids to see if you feature in any of them. Ring home to see if there is a media scrum outside. Make sure you didn't miss the vote last night.

If you are an optimist, you might think he is about to offer you a job on the Front Bench. Or, more likely and less enjoyable, he wants you to speak at his Association's Annual Dinner.

"There is a new line to take on Europe." This means the Party's policy has changed suddenly, to the dismay of those who had taken the trouble to find out what it was, and had been staunchly defending it.

"Division. Free Vote." Panic. When you get to the lobby, there will be no guidance from the Whips about how to vote. You have eight minutes in which to find someone who will summarise the issue fairly, without trying to get you to follow him into his own particular disposition.

"A very Happy Christmas to you all." This requires no explanation. The Whips are, contrary to popular belief, human and capable of expressing seasonal good wishes.
And so am I.

***

Negative Outcome

January 2008

With the House of Commons back at work, memories of Christmas and the New Year celebrations are receding fast. However, there is one consequence of the festive season that needs to be resolved.

The Young family are relatively organised when it comes to lists of who wants what for Christmas. (A list system promotes focussed giving and removes the risk of duplicated and unwanted gifts – and is much favoured in households run by economists.)

There was only one thing I really wanted this year, and this was a device that turns photographic negatives (remember them?) into digital images. I reckoned this would be useful because negatives degrade over time; and because it would promote the collocation of all photographs – digital and analogue - in a common and indestructible catalogue, suitable for generations of Youngs as yet unborn.

So I put this item on the list and made it clear that, in view of its cost, it would be acceptable for members of the family to form a syndicate and purchase it collectively.

Some discreet enquiries before Christmas revealed that my request had fallen on deaf ears and, whatever Santa would be bringing down the chimney on Christmas Day, a negative scanner with inbuilt software that normalises over-saturated colours would not be in the sack.

So, to avoid disappointment, I ordered it over the internet myself in the days before Christmas.

I was greeted with the following email.

"We know that holidays can be stressful and wanted to relieve a portion of that stress by reassuring you that your package should leave our Fulfilment Centre soon. Despite the slight delay, we expect your order to arrive in time for Christmas."

What you and I call a depot has been upgraded to a Fulfilment Centre. Where will this stop? The House of Commons will be a Manifesto Delivery Centre, my tax office a Disposable Income Redistribution Centre, the local District General Hospital a Health Restoration Centre.

The Fulfilment Centre disgorged my present before Christmas, and it was indeed exactly what I wanted. However, a second disappointment lay ahead. I discovered that, while tidying up the relevant drawers earlier in the year, another member of my household of whom I am very fond had thrown away nearly all the old negatives, leaving just the fading photographs in the yellow Kodak folders. A few had survived the cull, and their contents have been transferred into digital form and captured, labelled and dated for the benefits of future generations. But the machine with the software-based function for removing dust and scratches from treasured images was redundant.

Fortunately I had kept the box and, having tested Amazon, I was now on to eBay. No one would know that the unwanted Christmas present I was disposing of was one that I had bought for myself. As I write this, the auction is under way and a substantial capital write-off will be required when the gift leaves this fulfilment centre on its way to Esskaybee123, whose modest bid leads the field.

Walden Hour

July 2008

I have recently returned from a bonding weekend with my parliamentary colleagues. These innovative events were introduced to my Party by William Hague, who borrowed them from the corporate sector, - probably McKinseys - where he spent his formative years. They involve spending the weekend with the same people that you spend the week with, in the belief that, if you meet them wearing sweaters rather than suits, this will reveal hidden qualities which lead to enduring relationships. (Any gain has to be balanced against the loss of quality time with wife and family, who don't expect to see the MP during the week, but hope they might catch a glimpse of him during the weekend.)

One of the speakers at our bonding weekend was Brian Walden. Older readers will remember Brian as the Presenter of Weekend World; and even older readers will remember him as a Labour MP. He appeared at our weekend because he is a convert to my Party, having been won round by Margaret Thatcher. He spoke with vigour, humour and conviction and should be despatched to every marginal seat in the country to spread the gospel.

The last time I met him was on his programme. Nowadays, an interview on television lasts twenty seconds if you are a member of the public, three minutes if you are MP, and about 20 minutes if you are Prime Minister. On Weekend World in the 1980s, it lasted an hour if you were Minister for Housing. So anxious for me to appear on the programme were the organisers that they sent two cars to fetch me from my home on a Sunday, lest the first car carrying me broke down. (One car was provided for the return journey.)

Brian's technique was to break the interview down into about six component parts, for each of which he had a desired outcome. At the end of the interview, he would assemble the six desired outcomes, put them together and pronounce them to be a damning condemnation of whatever policy he was reviewing.

The only problem with the Walden technique was that the Minister he was interviewing probably knew more about the subject than Brian did (though this was not always the case). So the denouement would not always go as planned.

When this happened, he had another trick up his sleeve. The presenters of the programme wanted to extract something from the 60 minutes that the rest of the media would pick up as a story. Journalists writing on Sunday for Monday would watch the programme for inspiration – or for gaffes.

Thus it was that, after an innocuous reply from me to one of his questions, Brian paused, leant forward, and stabbed me with his finger. "Minister" he said "You have just said something vewy intewesting." "I want to pwess you on that a little further."

My heart froze. The last thing any Minister wants to hear on any political programme is that he has said something intewesting. Our whole professional training is focussed on avoiding saying anything at all. So I spent the rest of the programme convincing him that what I had said was devoid of any interest at all.

Today, Ministers have a new solution to avoiding saying anything interesting on television. They simply refuse to be interviewed.

***

Supermarket Competition

August 2008

Before I became the MP for North West Hampshire, I represented Ealing Acton – a constituency of beauty and contrast. All the beauty was in Ealing and all the contrast was in Acton. I remember attending the opening of a new supermarket in West London in the 1970s.

It was small by today's standards, but large for its time. I stood next to a gentleman whom I didn't recognise, but whose autograph was widely sought after by the ladies invited for the occasion (in those days, men on the whole didn't shop.) He was the villain in a soap opera, supplementing his income by cutting ribbons. Before the ceremony began, he asked me how much I had been paid to come along. I had to admit I had come along for nothing. (With my small majority, I was almost in the business of paying for photo opportunities such as these). He took a dim view of my low market value, regarding it as potentially depressing the fee which he could command. He kept on looking nervously at his script which said "I hereby declare this supermarket open." I thought, given his professional background, he might have been able to commit this sentence to memory. As the Towncrier, also hired for the occasion, commanded silence, he and I gazed round the cavernous metal windowless construction that lay before us. "I declare this supermarket open" declared the villainous Mr Soap; but then he began to ski off-piste "But all this stuff will have to go when they bring the aeroplanes back inside."

This throwaway remark caused him to go up considerably in my estimation. But the architect and the store manager were unamused. The store manager spoke to the soap star's agent, who I suspect had crafted the speech. It seemed that the fee was being renegotiated downwards, to that with which Members of Parliament are familiar.

It was the only supermarket opening I attended in 23 years in Ealing Acton. Since coming to Andover, I seem to do little else. Lidls; then Sainsbury's (when it took over from Safeway); then Asda; and now, to judge by the signs, Sainsbury's again.

This has led to a welcome burst of competition for the Andover purse. Vouchers are flying around the town, with supermarkets accepting each other's tokens. There are some ASDA flowerbeds at the Tesco roundabout, and Tesco should respond by buying the cinema above ASDA. The Consumer is King.

The latest round in these store wars has just arrived through my letterbox, imploring me to use my computer to buy my food on-line. One sentence of the many promises caught my eye "To deliver in perfect condition, picked and packed with passion by W**tr**e Partners"

How, I asked my wife (who still does the shopping) might we tell the difference between produce that is picked and packed with passion; and produce that is picked and packed without passion? Some lipstick on the cereal packet? A tear-stain on the croissants? Some tell-tale saliva on the frozen Chicken Masala?

Is there an option for those of us who prefer our food picked and packed in the English as opposed to the French style?

***

What is in a Name?

September 2008

Bicycling through Andover the other day, I noticed that there are now more fellow cyclists on the road, doubtless driven out of their cars by the high cost of petrol. This growth in two-wheeled traffic is accompanied by a welcome exercise by Test Valley Borough Council, who want to make the town a more cycle-friendly place. My thoughts about how to assist them were distracted when I saw a van belonging to a company that made garage doors. It had ingeniously combined the name of the town with the name of the product it promoted "Up-And-over Garage Doors" was emblazoned on the vehicle.

Could this lateral thinking not be more widely applied, I asked myself, harnessing pride in the town with some new names for the businesses that trade in it? I share my suggestions with readers, and will be looking for a response from the progressive thinkers in the trading community in the town.

Is there a market for a new bank in the town with the challenging title "Andover Your Money"? – or possibly in these challenging times "AndOverdraft"?; should we not have a fish restaurant invitingly called "AnDover Sole", next to a new pub (not that the town needs any more pubs) called "AndOverindulge?"

We already have two well-established undertakers, but I believe there is room for a third, "AndOver My Dead Body." Could Thruxton Airfield be renamed "LAndover There", and what about a new photocopying service " Over Andover Again?"

There don't seem to be many architects in the town, so a new firm called "Plandover" might find a ready market; and those who are worried about their pallour on the beach might patronise a sunbed shop called "Tannedover". And how about a new Boxing Club "Andover Fist"; and a Mens' Outfitter "AndOvercoat"; and a new pharmacy in the Chantry Centre "AndOverdose" ?

Could we have a rival for Stagecoach with a new bus service along the B3400 "Whitchurch AndOverton"; or, if you prefer the railway, a new service "AndOverground". If neither take off, we could take our custom to a new car-hire firm "AndOverdrive."

The new cinema, instead of being called Reels, could have been "Andover Head Projector" and a new bookshop could be called "AndOverleaf". The new Premier Inn by 100 Acre roundabout could have been "AndOverNight" and we could have a new travel company selling cruises "AndoverSeas."

I believe this particular seam has been well and truly quarried; work will stop before people start saying there is a room for a new MP.

Tribute to Art Buchwald

October 2008

I am grateful to the late and great Art Buchwald, the American humourist, for this explanation of how a recession starts – a phenomenon which economists are pleased to call the reverse multiplier.

The owner of Andover Garages, Geoffrey Silverstone, rang up one of his regular customers, Maurice Blake, who ran a gentleman's outfitters in the town. "Maurice, I'm just ordering some of the new Jaguars, and I'm earmarking one for you. What colour and when would you like it?"

"Sorry mate, no can do. Julie's left me and her sharp barrister is taking me to the cleaners. And I have had a letter from the CSA. Do you sell scooters?"

Geoffrey hung up but soon the phone rang. It was Henry Frostpane, of Output Joinery. "When can we come round to do your conservatory – we've just finished that job for the MP?"

"The deal's off." said Geoff. "But I've got all the panels." "Sorry Henry, but Maurice is not buying the Jag. I can't afford it now."

When Henry got home, he found his wife had bought a huge new plasma TV from Stan Widescreen. Fortunately, it was unwrapped. "That's going back to Stan in the morning" "Why so?" "Geoffrey's not building the conservatory, because Maurice isn't buying the Jag."

Stan's face fell when he got the TV back from Henry. He rang Philip Beachcomber at Andover Travel. "That holiday to Turkey, Phil? – I am afraid it's off." "But the tickets are here – with no fuel surcharge and take-off from Southampton." "Henry's not buying the TV set because Henry's not building Geoff's extension, because Maurice isn't buying the Jag."

Philip went round to Charles Portal, his bank manager. "I am afraid I can't make this month's repayment" "Stan's not buying his holiday because Henry's not buying a TV because Geoffrey doesn't want a conservatory, because Maurice isn't buying the Jag."

When Andrew Makepeace came in to borrow money for the extension to his nursing home, he got a flea in his ear from Charles. "I can't lend you any money because Philip has missed this month's repayment." Andrew rang up Norman Brown, the builder, who laid off eight men.

A few week's later, Jaguar slashed the prices on their new models. Geoffrey rang up Maurice. " At these prices, even you can afford one – after the divorce costs."

"Oh that's all over. There was a misunderstanding – Julie's back. The 'other man' really was a plumber fixing the taps in the ensuite.

"Then you can certainly afford the car."

"You must be joking. Trade is flat on its face. I haven't seen you, Henry, Stan, Phil, Charles, Andrew or Norman in my shop for weeks."

***

Parliamentary Football Team

October 2008

Last Saturday afternoon was spent at the Madejski Stadium in Reading, watching Reading play Queens Park Rangers. I drove there with mixed loyalties.

As a young lad growing up in Berkshire, I would make the pilgrimage on a Saturday to Elm Park Road – their old ground - to watch Reading play at home. Known then as the Biscuitmen, because of the Huntley and Palmer factory in the town, they never achieved the ambitions I harboured for them. I was subjected to cruel jokes by my friends who supported glamorous clubs like Arsenal and Spurs. They would ask me if it was true that, so small was the home crowd, the announcer read out the names of the spectators rather than the players. And was it the case that the Reading goalkeeper was so short-sighted that he couldn't even find the ball at the back of the net?

Later, as the MP for Acton in West London, I shared my commitment to Reading with a commitment to Queens Park Rangers. This was not as difficult as it sounds. They were in different leagues, and both sides had white and blue colours. Both were known as the Hoops and the cry from both terraces was the same – "Come On You R's". I bought four season tickets for myself and my two sons, who could then invite whichever schoolfriend they wanted to curry favour with. I started taking them at an early age – one son surprised his mother on return by singing a chant he had picked up from the terraces at Loftus Road - "The ref's a w*nker". Queens Park Rangers got to Wembley one year and lost, and then sank down the league. At one home game where they were playing appallingly, a dog strayed onto the pitch. The game was momentarily halted. "Leave the dog on" shouted my neighbour, "Take Masson off."

The game last Saturday was a draw, with QPR thankful to get an away point, having sacked their manager the day before.

I played my last game of football a few years ago for the parliamentary team. We went to Bisham Abbey, where the England team trained, to play a team of Swiss Parliamentarians. We were hoping to get revenge for the Annual Ski Race at Davos which the Swiss Parliamentarians understandably won every year.

We played this match after a bitter row in the Commons, when the Labour Government were accused of breaking a pair – the equivalent of pocketing your opponent's ball at golf. Relations had broken down and, if MPs had ambassadors, they would have been recalled. We took to the pitch barely on speaking terms with each other and perhaps took our row to extremes. The Conservatives would only pass to other Conservatives, and the Labour MPs would only pass to other comrades. By half-time, we were severely behind. After sucking an orange, we agreed to call a truce and went on to win.

***

The Regions

November 2008

This column does not normally record my activities in Parliament. If they are significant, they will be reported in the serious papers. If they are scandalous, they will appear in the tabloids.

But, earlier this month, I had a minor triumph which constituents are entitled to know about. This fell neither into the significant nor scandalous category and therefore passed unnoticed.

Eight years ago, the Government established a Committee of the English Regions. At the time, speaking from the Opposition Front Bench on behalf of my Party, I predicted that this was an unnecessary measure and urged the House to oppose it. In my view, there is no appetite for a regional dimension. If I talk about Wessex to my constituents, they think about Edward and Sophie – not a tier of government.

I was put in my place by the Leader of the House, who told me that "such a forum will add usefully to the procedures of the House."

So useful was the Committee that it has not met in the five years since April 2003. Indeed, so insignificant is its contribution to the good governance of the country that, in this Parliament, the Government has not even bothered to appoint members to sit on it.

Week after week, for the past three and a half years, a Committee on which I sit has invited the Government to nominate members to this committee, and each week nominations were there none.

I dislike clutter, and am a committed de-regulator.

Might, I suggested to the Government, this committee be abolished and laid to rest? I would be happy to deliver an appropriate tribute over its grave – necessarily a short tribute, because of its modest achievements. This pill was too bitter for the Government to swallow.

Two weeks ago, there was a window of opportunity. There was to be a debate and some resolutions on Select Committees; I tabled an amendment to delete the Committee of the English Regions and spoke powerfully to it. It was a short speech, as, in an affront to democracy, the Government had guillotined the debate. Not a voice was raised in defence of the Committee of the Regions, and, as the vote drew near, I asked the Government if they would accept my amendment. No, I was told; the Minister thought the committee might yet serve a useful purpose. I contacted my friends in the Labour Party, who shared my view about the efficacy of this, and the Government faced the possibility of defeat in the lobbies.

At the crucial moment, they withdrew their opposition and my amendment was carried, unopposed.

My elation was short-lived. In the next vote, the Government set up eight new regional committees to replace the single English Committee of the Regions I had just abolished.

In eight years time, if not before, I anticipate that these too will meet a similar fate.

I am polishing my amendment in anticipation.

The Christmas Present

December 2008

It is a sign of advancing years that one finds policemen are getting younger. I suffer from a related symptom, finding that Father Christmases are getting younger. This disappointment has been blunted by finding that, unlike every other Christmas, the goods I am looking at in the shops are going down in price rather than up. I would have done some shopping last week in Woolworths before it closed for good, but didn't have half a day to spend in the queue at checkout.

The fundamentals of Christmas shopping have changed dramatically. As a child, I knew exactly what I wanted, but didn't know what to give other people. Now I know exactly what to give other people, (because they are good enough to tell me); but I don't know what I want. I already have a goodly number of spare rear lights for my bicycle, and I had been given six 2009 diaries before the beginning of December. I have a drawer full of mouse mats, more paintings than space to hang them, calendars from almost every village in North West Hants, tea towels and commemorative mugs from schools and churches.

The immediate problem is what to buy my wife. As she occasionally reads my articles, there are restrictions on what I can say without diminishing her excitement on December 25th.

She has asked for a new ******** to replace the one which I passed on to her three years ago, when I bought myself a new one. She would like it to be faster and quieter than the one she has now, and to break down less often.

So I put ******** into a search engine and ordered a 2008 model with a large ***** and extra *** for £***.99. It has a low carbon footprint, low energy costs, a long life-cycle and additional security features.

My order was rejected because the delivery address was different from the address at which my credit card is registered. It generated a call from fraud control, which had to be answered before an important line of credit was cut off.

I then ordered the same model from *m*z*n, but at £***.99 plus £**. They did not have the same sensitivities about which address they delivered to and accepted the order.

Two days later, they apologised. Their stock control system was at fault. The ******** was not in stock, and the next delivery to them would take place on December 24th . Unless it was put straight onto Santa's sleigh, it was unlikely to arrive in time. I was given the option of cancelling the order, which I did. But while *m*z*n's stock control system was at fault, its system for extracting money from my bank account had worked perfectly.

Now I will have to go to *****'s in ****** Street, Andover and get her a c**k**y b**k.

***

The Tax Return

January 2009

The newspapers contain constant reminders telling us that, by January 31st, those who haven't already sent in their tax return must do so; if they don't, they will be fined to help the Government service the national debt.

My Ministerial career had a few moments of excitement, one of which was the privatisation of the country's railways. (Despite offers of clemency, I have refused to plead guilty to any offence.) But I was also the Minister who introduced self-assessment for the nation's taxpayers.

My partner in the mission to sell self-assessment was Hector the Inspector. Older readers may remember seeing on their screens in

1996 a portly, bowler-hatted cartoon figure, whose trousers were held up by braces. This was Hector.

When I first heard about the campaign, I asked to see the advertisements. I was extremely worried. The Government of which I was a member had already managed to upset important sections of the electorate (as the 1997 election was shortly to show) and I was reluctant to add to this list the employees of Inland Revenue by publicly lampooning them. I had never seen any of the men wear a bowler hat; it would have been an impertinence to enquire as to what held up their trousers; and, while some had a Body Mass Index that would have raised a doctor's eyebrow, they were not generically obese.

I asked my office to summon the shop steward of the nation's tax collectors to the Treasury to get his reaction to the TV commercial. He was delighted by it. It portrayed the tax inspector as a jovial character, not averse to a pint in the local after dishing out tax rebates all day. Neither he nor his members would object.

So we launched Hector. After the film Silence of the Lambs, and as the Revenue got tougher, I gather Hector became commonly known as Lecter.

Hector was pensioned off in 2001, having been described by the Chairman of the Inland Revenue as having "got out of control."

Before I finally decided to inflict self-assessment on the nation, I decided to have a go at the forms myself. They arrived on my desk in the Treasury, and I took in to the office the data I had used for my last tax return. I asked to be left undisturbed until I either gave up, had to phone a friend or ask the audience. In 40 minutes the form was completed. Hector had a look at my work and pronounced it fit for purpose. And so, in 1997, self-assessment was launched, along with the ability to file on-line.

Which is what most people now do. But this facility is denied to its author. The security of the online computer system, used by more than three million people to file tax returns, is in doubt after HM Revenue and Customs admitted it was not properly secure. So along with those deemed by the Revenue to be "celebrities" and the Royal Family, Members of Parliament still have to send their return by post.

**

Blessing or Blight?

February 2009

Forty years ago, as a young man with a wife, two children and a Labrador to support, I was approached by Penguin Books and asked to write a book in a series they were doing on popular geography. They would pay me £400, and I would liaise with Prof Peter Hall, Professor of Geography at the University of Reading. I would write the book, and he would write the Foreword.

I was moderately busy, with a full-time job as Economic Adviser to the Post Office Corporation, and two part-time jobs as a councillor on the London Borough of Lambeth (with Cllr John Major), and as a member of the Greater London Council (which I subsequently helped to abolish). My parliamentary ambitions were on hold, as Conservative Central Office had indicated that, in their view, I did not have the necessary qualities to represent the Party in the House of Commons.

My book, "Tourism, Blessing or Blight?" was published two years later. It looked at the environmental and social implications of unconstrained growth of tourism, and it was bitterly attacked by the British Tourist Authority. Its Chairman at the time was Sandy Glen – aptly named for someone whose job it was to promote travel to attractive destinations. Though I say it myself, it was slightly ahead of its time.

My book cost the discerning buyer 40p, in the newly decimalised currency. 15,000 copies were printed, and 15,000 discerning buyers bought them all within weeks. However, no further copies were ever printed, for reasons I never understood. The Penguin lady I had negotiated with was on the commissioning side of the business, and the sell-out of the book had vindicated her judgement in backing this unheard-of author. The sales and printing people worked in a different building, and they didn't seem to communicate.

No royalty cheques ever arrived, and the £400 went quickly on nappies and dog food. I decided not to become an author.

I thought no more of my book until Daughter No. 2 went to University 25 years later. She read Tourism, and found that my book was on her reading list. The book itself was unavailable, and those who wanted to gain enlightenment from it had to read photocopies in the library. My daughter told me, politely, that she had not found it an easy read. However, quotations from it appeared from time to time in the examination papers.

A sequel was written in 1999 "Tourism Reassessed: Blight or Blessing?" which its author kindly says was "inspired by" my important work.

Again, the book vanished from my thoughts until last week, when a fellow MP asked if he could read a copy. When I went home and looked through the shelves, no copy was to be found.

Nowadays, you can buy everything on the internet, so I did a spot of surfing. Sure enough, there is a market in the book. I could buy a copy – for the princely sum of £50. From 40p to £50 in forty years is a better investment than anything else in my portfolio. With my £400, I should have bought 1,000 copies, which would now be worth £50,000. That would have been a real blessing.

An Old Friend

March 2009

A few days ago, I came across an old friend. We had spent many dinner parties in each other's company and, after the port had circulated, he had brought amusement to those present. He even got me into the final round for the selection of a Parliamentary Candidate in Nottingham Central in the early 1970's. But I hadn't seen him for about ten years.

The old friend was at the bottom of my intray – a yellowing piece of paper called "The Joke". I had cut it out from a periodical in the 1960's, as it had made me laugh. I used it in speeches and it made others laugh. Eventually, the piece of paper began to fall to bits, and a kind secretary in whichever Department I was in at the time typed up several copies. She labelled them "The Joke" in case anyone confused the piece of paper for a serious Ministerial address. One copy lived inside my dinner jacket pocket, and was brought out whenever I had to sing for my supper.

Either I got tired of my old friend, or I reckoned that everyone had heard of him, so he was laid to rest in the in-tray some time ago. The in-tray is being spring-cleaned and before I finally bury him in Test Valley's brown recycling bin, I give him one last outing.

It tells the story of the Minister who muddled up his replies to parliamentary questions.

One question was "Is the Minister aware of the extensive damage done by rabbits, and will he take vigorous measures to have them eliminated?"

The other question was "May I direct the attention of the Minister to the increase in the number of Inspectors and other departmental officials, and urge him to check their multiplication?"

Both questions are as fresh today as they were then.

The wretched Minister, long before Jim Hacker appeared on anyone's screen, got them muddled up. To the first question about the rabbits, he replied as follows:

"No Sir. I believe that they are rendering valuable service to farmers, and that their activities should be welcomed and encouraged."

And to the second about the Inspectors, he replied "I am fully aware of the damage done by these pests, which are breeding at an alarming rate, and farmers are constantly being urged to exterminate them. Sporadic shooting is ineffectual and organised drives should be arranged at frequent intervals. It must however be remembered that they add variety to the countryman's diet, and that their fur has a certain market value."

Farewell, my dear friend. We had some good times together, and you served me well. Perhaps someone will exhume you, and may you then bring laughter to a future generation.

*Postcript. I updated this in the light of concern about Bovine Tuberculosis.

One question was "Is the Minister aware of the damage done to the country's dairy farmers by badgers, and will he take vigorous measures to reduce their numbers?"

The other question was "What action is the Minister taking to halt the increase in the number of civil servants at DEFRA?"

Sadly the Minister, new to the job, muddled the answers up. To the question about the badgers he replied "No Sir. I believe that they are rendering a valuable service to farmers, and that their activities should be welcomed and encouraged."

And to the second about the civil servants, he replied "I am fully aware of the damage done by these pests, which are breeding at an alarming rate and have no natural predators. Measures are in place to exterminate them as humanely as possible in Gloucestershire and Somerset. It must however be remembered that they added variety to the country's diet during the war, and that their hair can be used for quality shaving brushes."

Members' Interests

March 2009

Last month, I spent an hour driving to the home of a fellow MP. When I got there, he went to his chicken-run and gave me half a dozen newly laid eggs in a paper bag. I then got into his car and we drove, very carefully, for thirty minutes to the venue of a function whose guests I was to address. I spent thirty minutes before the meal talking politely to them about bovine tuberculosis, the prospects for the English Cricket Team and the fine weather. We then adjourned to a barn that had been converted into an art gallery, where I spent an hour eating a good three course meal. I cannot remember what was discussed, as I was wondering what on earth I would say when, after the meal, silence was prayed for the Rt Hon Member for North West Hants.

I addressed the company for 20 minutes, the first five of which were spent, as custom requires, singing the praises of whoever's constituency I find myself in. During my address, three people went to sleep. I answered questions for a further twenty minutes – including the statutory one as to why we weren't a more effective Opposition - and was then presented with a bottle of Bollinger Special Cuvée Champagne. I then took 90 minutes to get home, wondering if I could persuade my wife to scramble the eggs and open the champagne, so we could have a proper breakfast in the morning.

Why do I tell you this? Because I have to. We have tightened up the rules for the Register of Members' Interests, and we have to reveal outside earnings, and the amount of time we spend earning them.

I happen to be a full-time MP with no outside earnings, but I approve of MPs bringing their experience to our debates, and am wary of a House of Commons composed exclusively of a political class reared in a hothouse of Student Unions, Think Tanks and Special Adviserships. However, the definition of "earnings" apparently includes the home-laid eggs and the bottle of champagne. The question I have to ask myself, confronted with the form for the Register of Members' Interests, is "Would I have been given the eggs and champagne, if I hadn't made the speech?" The answer is obviously no. So I earned them. And as there is no "de minimis" limit –all earnings, however small, have to be declared. So the eggs and the champagne are in the Register. Along with the time I spent earning them.

The good news is that I don't get paid for writing columns for the local paper, so I won't have to declare it. Nor indeed will I have to declare the time it took me to write it.

But, since you are interested, 14 minutes 37 seconds – the length of the second movement of Schubert's 9th Symphony, interpreted by Leonard Bernstein, which inspired it. And that includes time off to make a cup of tea, finish yesterday's Times Crossword, take a photograph of the duck in the garden, and clean my fingernails.

***

The Budget Statement

April 2009

When I first started paying tax, Tax Freedom Day was April 24th . Tax Freedom Day is the totemic date in the Adam Smith Calendar, when the citizen stops working for the Government and begins working for himself. (The self-employed sadly cannot beat the system by only working from April 24th, nor can the tax exile escape by only coming here after that date, and leaving on December 31st.)

Before taking my seat to listen to this year's Budget, I established that Tax Freedom Day last year was June 2nd – itself a comment on how the tentacles of the state have grown during my time as a taxpayer. After listening to the Chancellor for 45 minutes, the Government won't be going to the IMF in 2010 to borrow some money; it will be going to 2011 to borrow some more time. I am going to have to work longer for the Government than there are days in the year, and the Adam Smith calendar will have to be redesigned. I was encouraged by the variation on this theme from Al Murray who said "Not until about halfway through your pint do you stop drinking for the Government and start drinking for yourself."

And so the ritual of the Budget is over for another year. Colleagues stopped turning up in morning suits with carnations in their buttonholes some time ago, and the ladies have stopped wearing hats. It is a monochrome occasion, and this was not an exciting Budget. The Chancellor didn't even pause to drink some whisky-coloured fluid before announcing the increase in duty on spirits – traditionally one of the lighter moments in the Budget speech.

During one of Nigel Lawson's Budgets, I was sitting next to one of the wealthier MPs, who was keeping the score on his pocket calculator. As the personal allowances were increased, he would score a plus of the relevant sum; as the duty on alcohol increased, he would score a minus. When Child Benefit went up, he was up, and when petrol duty went up, he was down again. By the end of the Budget, he was marginally up on the proceedings and was about to put the calculator away.

Nigel then announced a reduction in the top rate of tax of 40%. My colleague tapped away, and then a look of bewilderment came over him. "What's the matter?" I asked.

"There aren't enough noughts on this machine to tell me the value of that change."

The All Party Cycling Group

April 2009

I am not a great one for using the parliamentary recess to go abroad with my colleagues, of whom I see a lot during the sessions. In fact, the last time I went on an overseas delegation was in 1990 when I went to Belize with John Prescott. Hurricane Diana brought our visit to a dramatic close and it has taken me 19 years to pluck up the courage to go on another one.

I am Patron of the All Party Parliamentary Cycling Group, who planned a two day fact-finding visit to Holland during the Easter Recess. Cycling is one of my special subjects and I am interested in seeing how we can learn from others who have a better record than we have. So I dug out the passport, found some euros left over from a holiday in Italy, packed my cycle clips and turned up at St Pancras to catch the Eurostar with other members of the APPCG.

The Dutch have a natural advantage over the British. In the Beginning, when the Almighty created Heaven and Earth, he made part of the earth flat. This was the part that the Dutch decided to colonise and grow tulips on, (unaware that it was below sea-level and that, in due course, the icebergs which the Almighty created later in the week would melt and flood them.) The British chose the other side of the Channel, where you get better views and stay dry for longer.

This geological diversity accounts for the difference in cycle penetration. The Dutch have 1.1 bicycle per Dutch man, woman and child, and the bicycles are used every day. We Brits have one bicycle for every two people and most of them are kept safe in the garden shed until the tanker drivers or railway workers go on strike.

Cyclists in this country tend to be male, under 40 and to dress for it. Most cyclists in Holland are women, and for them it is just like walking. There are so many cyclists that car drivers there are like cyclists in London – a persecuted minority who have to fight to stay on the road.

We spent much of our time with Dutch Railways. Whereas Network Rail uses the space at or near its stations for revenue generating activities, such as Burger King, Dutch Railways use it for the free parking of bicycles. And if a passenger doesn't own a bicycle, the Dutch station master will rent you one. 40% of those who catch the train in Holland arrive at the station on a bicycle.

At the end of our tour, which included a bicycle ride round the Hague in the rain, our hosts dropped us at a railway station so we could return to the Land where Car is King. We had forty-five minutes before departure, and we wanted to sit down for a cup of coffee and to dry out. We looked round the six platforms in vain; and then round the rest of the station. Then we walked a quarter of a mile past two thousand bicycles until we found a Starbucks.

Forecasting the Winners

April 2009

Readers may be familiar with the operation of the Pools Panel. This body of football aficianados are invited to guess what might have happened, had the weather not prevented a particular fixture from taking place. (The original Pools Panel in 1963 comprised Sir Gerald Nabarro (a moustachio'd Conservative backbench MP), George Young (no relation - an ex–Scottish International) and the Tommies Lawton and Finney.

Supplied with the relevant statistics and a good lunch, they forecast the result of the postponed games for the benefit of those who played the pools; or, more accurately, for the benefit of those who operated the pools.

This pragmatic approach to the unpredictable intervention of the Almighty is now being extended to the field of education. Exam boards, I read, are working on contingency plans to award children GCSE and A-level grades, based on coursework and marks from modules already sat, if they are unable to attend an exam because of swine flu.

In the words of the Minister "There are already procedures in place if candidates can't sit their exams and are given special consideration. These can be put into action if things get worse. In contingency terms, all these things are being discussed by exam boards."

But why stop at exams? What happens, I ask myself, if the Prime Minister were to summon up the courage to invite Her Majesty to dissolve Parliament, and, between dissolution and polling day, the World Health Authority raised the pandemic level of swine flu to six, and we were all confined to our homes with face masks and packets of Tamiflu? It would not be possible to postpone the General Election; that requires a change in the law, and there would be no one entitled so to do. Canvassing and voting would be banned by COBRA, master-minding operations from a germ-free bunker in Whitehall.

Assuming the election is held when the football season is over, I believe we should invite the Pools Panel to intervene and decide the outcome. Candidates would submit the relevant information on form (in my case, played nine, won nine and appearing in front of a home crowd). But of course others would be allowed to submit their own case and the decision of the panel would be final. At 5pm on a Saturday, James Alexander Gordon would be enticed out of retirement to read the results. The appropriate Party Leader, who would be over the moon, would go off to the Palace to collect the trophy and the Leader of the Opposition would be sick as a parrot.

If it works, we might raise our sights. The next time a war looks imminent, the Pools Panel could declare the winner, without a shot being fired.

***

Is Mr Young in this Division?

May 2009

When I was at school, eleven o'clock was an important time. If you were to be summoned to the Headmaster's Study for some misdemeanour, that was the time when you got the call. And it was dramatic.

A young man in a morning suit, coloured silk waistcoat, winged collar and white bow tie would burst into the class. "Is Mr X in this division?" he would demand, fortissimo. Or, occasionally, for this was Eton, "Is Lord Y in this division?" The beak, who was explaining the significance of early political satire in The Frogs by Aristophanes, would then admit wearily to the presence of the afore-mentioned pupil. "He is required to attend the Headmaster in his study at midday" the silk waistcoat would declaim. A silence would descend on the class, as the implications of the summons were absorbed; the colour would drain from Mr X's face; and then it was back to Aristophanes and his satire, with a wry chuckle from the beak.

Depending on the severity of the offence, the punishment was the writing out of thousands of lines of Latin verse – Virgil's Georgics; or the cane.

If eleven o'clock came and went, and there was no summons, then you were OK. The dalliance with the Housemaster's daughter the previous evening had been unobserved. No doubt it has all changed now; any summons is done by text message; corporal punishment has been abolished and anger management is prescribed for any misdemeanours.

50 years later, eleven o'clock has the same significance. If the Member of Parliament has not heard from The Telegraph about his expenses by 11am, he knows that he is OK for another day. Punishment is not imminent.

Last Thursday, I was on the train back to the constituency, doing the Times Crossword, when my mobile went at 11am. "This is the Daily Telegraph."

It was the "Is Mr Young in this division?" moment. The colour drained from my face. A fellow passenger passed over his plastic bottle of water, noticing my distress. The Telegraph wanted an email address to which to send a communication about an article they proposed to publish about me the following day. I gave the email address – which they already had – and got the laptop down from the luggage rack to find out the worst.

The rest is history. I was splashed all over the paper the next day, photographed on a bicycle and excoriated for my extravagance in replacing a broken washing-machine in my London flat with a new one from the John Lewis Partnership.

I sat by my computer, waiting for North West Hants to erupt digitally. But my constituents are either a forgiving lot, or they already know the worst about their Member. I had one email of complaint. It was from someone who was appalled – that I was not wearing a crash helmet on my bicycle. It was the Georgics, rather than the cane.

***

Changing Stations

June 2009

At the last election, or was it the one before, the slogan was "Vote Blue, Go Green." It underlined my party's commitment to save the planet for future generations. So the Young household takes steps to minimise its carbon footprint. The garage is packed with bicycles; the kitchen is full of different coloured bins; the deep-freeze is crammed with home-grown fruit and vegetables; the garden has water-butts and a compost box - and the boot of the car is full of empty bottles (from when the children came to stay, you understand) awaiting delivery to the Charlton Recycling Centre.

Sharing the garage with the bicycles is a car which says it does "up to" 70 miles to the gallon. (Not all journeys in a constituency 30 miles by 15 can be done on two wheels.) The car was acquired recently and its previous owner was addicted to popular music. He had pre-tuned the radio to every channel playing top of the pops. It has been possible to add some extra stations – R*d*os 3 and 4, and C*a*s*c FM – but moving between these three involves going through all the other channels, while one's eyes are focussed on the A303. Surely, I said, it must be possible to eradicate the preset stations that are surplus to requirements, leaving the small number of ones that are essential to my in-car entertainment, including of course Andover Sound. Not so.

Although it has 576 pages, the handbook sheds no light on how stations can be deleted, only how more can be added. (But it does tell me how to clean the seatbelts.) A quick visit to Google revealed that other owners had encountered the same problem, and been unable to delete from their car's memory the musical tastes of the last owner. The only way to solve the problem, according to the handbook, was to remove the relevant fuse from the fusebox, and start again.

Pages 436 to 446 of the handbook explain how to do this. There are two fuse boxes in the car. One easily accessible under the bonnet; and one less accessible in the passenger's footwell. Fuse 29 is in the footwell. The fuse box is not on the side of the footwell, but on the underneath of the dashboard. To access it, you have to lie down, resting your head in the footwell, gazing up with the help of a torch. If you are very small, you might be able to curl up in the foetal position in the footwell, and proceed; but if you are of conventional dimensions, you have to get a mattress for the lower half of the body outside the car, while the top half is in the car.

Finding the fuse is not easy. And, having found it, removing it is like a dentist removing the pin that holds in place the crown of a tooth. Except the dentist can do this in comfort sitting on a stool. I reached the last line of the instructions. "Remove the fuse with the pull-out tool." But nowhere are you told where the pull-out tool lives.

So the journey from R*d*o 3 to C*a*s*c FM remains punctuated by 30 seconds of p*p.

Liaison Committee

July 2009

If you asked a politics graduate, working on a doctorate on the centralisation of power in 21st century Britain, what he would like for his birthday, he might well answer – two and a half hours with the Prime Minister. Although this was not on my list of wants, that is how I spent my birthday last week. On the basis of a ten hour working day, I spent a quarter of it with the Prime Minister. And with nineteen other Select Committee Chairmen. And with whomever was tuned in to the Parliament Channel and lasted the course.

I mean no disrespect to our current Prime Minister (Gordon Brown) when I say these sessions are less animated than the ones with his predecessor, who would engage more readily in spirited exchanges.

The challenge for the Select Committee Chairmen with Tony Blair was to get him to address us by our Christian names before our sequence of questions came to an end. His use of that familiarity was a signal that our questioning was getting close to the mark. When the session was over, like fighter pilots returning to base in the Second World War, we would compare scores and award medals.

We are having to change the rules with Gordon. In his first reply, before I had even warmed up, he had called me Sir George.

These exchanges require some preparation. You know you can only ask a certain number of questions, and the later ones depend on the answers to the earlier ones. Lines of retreat need to be blocked off.

My strategy was simple yet, to my mind, cunning. It was to confront the Prime Minister with what the newly-elected Speaker had said about Prime Minister's Questions, and ask him if he agreed.

To understand the subtlety of this strategy, readers need to know the relevant quotation, which I reproduce here.

"The Punch and Judy show is boring, extremely abrasive and is now a contributory factor to the contempt bordering on opprobrium in which we are now held."

Whatever his reply, I calculated, the Prime Minister was in trouble.

If he agreed with the Speaker's analysis, I would then accuse him of being complicit in bringing politics into disrepute. As the principal performer at Prime Minister's Questions, he could hardly distance himself from how it was conducted.

If, on the other hand, he challenged the Speaker's analysis, I could accuse him of a constitutional impropriety of the highest order, by challenging the opinion of the man who conducts the proceedings in the House.

How could he avoid this carefully contrived trap, once I had covered it with sticks and leaves?

Readers may have guessed what happened. He made a large detour and failed to answer the question.

I reproduce below his non-monosyllabic reply from Hansard.

Mr Brown: Well, I would like to see the House of Commons distinguish itself by being able to deal with, often in a non-party-political way, some of the big issues of our time. Prime Minister's Question Time has not ever been, as far as I can see in the time that I have been in, the vehicle for that to happen. I think the sadness about the House of Commons is that there are very big issues our country faces and, whether it is Afghanistan or whether it is issues that go right across to assisted dying that are moral issues that people are worried about, we do not seem to be able to find the vehicles by which these issues can be debated in a way that commends itself to the country.

Ah well, it was worth a go.

Recalled to the Colours

September 2009

Two weeks ago, Aurelia and I left for a six day holiday in Croatia. We had planned to leave just after the August Bank Holiday with the last of the summer fêtes behind us, and to come back to England before the two countries played each other in the World Cup. We did this in case the warm Croatian hospitality became chilled in the event of an England win; or we found ourselves surrounded in Dubrovnik by rejoicing locals offering us commiserations.

I assumed the high point of the holiday had been on the first day, when we travelled out in the same plane as the Saint and James Bond – a youthful-looking Roger Moore sitting several rows in the aircraft ahead of us, behind a curtain. "Isn't that Sean Connery?" asked a passenger as she went past, running the risk of being annihilated by a bullet fired from a biro designed by Q.

Our plans in Croatia were for a rest, some gentle travel, a brush with local culture and a search for early works by Aurelia's father – the sculptor Oscar Nemon. We didn't plan to be in constant communication with our native land. So no laptop – just the occasional visit to an internet café to keep ahead of the game. And a mobile phone left at the hotel, and switched on in the evening to see if there were any messages. It was a formula appropriate for an unimportant Opposition backbencher that had worked well in the past.

And thus it was that on September 7th, we were cruising round some sunkist off-shore islands and inhaling the smell of the grilled mackerel that the ship's crew were serving for lunch on board. Meantime, my Party leader was reshaping his Front Bench. I am not one who sits by the telephone during reshuffles. Indeed, I had been asked on local radio a few days earlier whether I anticipated a return to front-line politics and I had confidently replied that I had seen the inside of my last red box.

Unbeknownst to me, while we cruised from Sipan to Lopud, and swam in the sea, multiple messages were heading down the Adriatic. We got back in the evening to find a stack of SMS's on the mobile phone; backed up by some voicemail messages; reinforced by a pile of emails in the internet café and, for good measure, a fax pushed under the door by the hotelier. And, apparently, an emissary from the British Embassy diplomatically scouring the streets for us. All with the same message, but with mounting urgency as the hours passed. To ring my Party Leader.

I did so and the rest is history. Recalled to the colours. Back to the Shadow Cabinet table as Shadow Leader of the House. Embraced by collective responsibility. Given a slot at the Party Conference. Put up on the Today Programme to be lightly grilled by Humphreys.

And ordered never to move again without taking my Blackberry.

***

Security

October 2009

In a few days time, a group of politically motivated men and women will be heading from North West Hants up to Manchester for the Conservative Party Conference. I will be among them and will be staying there for five days. The last time I stayed in that great city was in 1993 when, as a Minister, I was backing its campaign to host the Olympics. My task, along with Bob Scott, was to persuade members of the International Olympic Committee that Manchester was the preferred destination for the games, despite the rain. They – and in some cases, their wives as well - enjoyed much hospitality and then they voted for Sydney.

I have kept the tie we commissioned for that campaign, which I propose to wear with pride. As Transport Secretary in 1996, I approved the building of a second runway for the airport. It was generously reported as the most significant construction project for Manchester since the opening of the Ship Canal in 1894. A number of people took a contrary view and headed for the trees in Arthurs Wood in order to obstruct the project. I also gave the go-ahead to the Metrolink extension to Salford Quays and Eccles, for which subsequent administrations have taken the credit. Whether my hosts recollect my commitment to the city's infrastructure remains to be seen, but they have kindly sent me, and all other attendees, a pass that gets me free travel on bus, train and tram. Previous party conferences have had their moments of excitement. At one, the Blackpool Constabulary contacted my office to ask for my inside leg measurements. My office were accustomed to mischievous enquiries from the press, but not from the arm of the law. "Why" they enquired "was this personal information needed?"

It turned out that I had chained my bicycle to the railings near the Imperial Hotel, and the frame might have been filled with gelignite. To ensure this was not the case, the saddle had been removed and an endoscopy carried out. Incipient traces of rust were found but otherwise it got a clean bill of health. Discreet enquiries and interrogation of the CCTV cameras had disclosed that the owner of the bicycle was the then Member for Ealing Acton. The reason for the phone call was that the police wished to leave the bicycle as they had found it. They needed to know my inside leg measurement to ensure that the saddle was the appropriate height from the ground (which meant that a normal sized adult needed a step ladder to get on to it.)

On an earlier occasion, a British Embassy overseas was concerned that the Foreign Secretary might not get through a revolving door. They telephoned his Private Office and asked a question of similar intrusiveness. "What is the diameter of the Foreign Secretary?" I am afraid we don't know his diameter." said the Private Secretary. "But we can tell you his circumference."

The Birth Centre

October 2009

Before heading north to Manchester last week for the Party Conference, I went to the Andover Birth Centre for its Open Day. Just as the two main political parties have recruited to their ranks experienced personnel from the Armed Forces, so, less controversially, I was joined on this visit by my wife. She has front line experience of matters maternal, whereas I am better on the theory than the practice. She talked intelligently to the midwives about breech deliveries while I asked the expectant mums about the birthing pool.

We have four children, but my wife has delivered five, the fifth being a grandson who was born in the back of my car. Daughter No. 1 was staying with us when she informed us that, while the confinement of her second child was not imminent, it was on the horizon. She wanted to be back in London with her nominated midwife, so we popped her in the back of the car and headed east. From the sounds behind me as we bowled along the A303, it was clear that the horizon was getting closer by the minute. I offered her the services of the Royal Hampshire Hospital in Winchester; then a few miles later, those of the North Hampshire Hospital in Basingstoke; and then a range of maternity units on either side of the M3. No, all was well.

By the time we reached the outskirts of London however, all was not well. I was instructed to bring the car to a halt and dial 999. I worked out which of the three emergency services we needed and, when connected, was asked where I was. It was, as they say, a good question. But it was one to which there was no immediate answer. I was on a dual carriageway on the south west corner of the capital, on one of those roads which carried no name and with no obvious landmark. And night had fallen.

While my dialogue was taking place, a grandson was delivered by my wife on the backseat of the car. I looked straight ahead and tuned in to Radio 3, having been told that this was a drama in which I had no useful part to play. The next day a colleague heard of the saga and asked how everything was. "Fine." I replied "Not a stain on the upholstery."

The young lad is now 10 and his second name is that of the car – Sterling. He is grateful that he was born before we bought our Toyota.

The Virus

November 2009

"I am sorry" are difficult words. Even more difficult, it is said, for politicians. And, when politicians do say them, it is sometimes to apologise for mistakes made by others, as when the Prime Minister apologised for the Irish potato famine and for the slave trade. They are words which I now address to many of my constituents.

Last week my wife sent me an email. Nothing unusual about that, but this one was not a confidential twitter from wife to husband, but an email sent to all those in her address book.

It began "Hi, Friend". It was re-assuring for me to read this, as it confirmed what I had hoped, namely that our relationship was an amicable one. But it then went on to ask "How are you doing recently?" And to inform me that she would "like to give me a big surprise." A Visa statement after another shopping expedition, possibly.

But the more I read, the clearer it was that this was not a communication from my wife, but from a third party who had hijacked her internet account The exhortation to log on to another website and buy a motorbike with a good after-sales service was the final give-away. I used to have two motorbikes, one each end of the railway line, but that stopped forty years ago under strong marital pressure.

My wife, who was on a lecture tour in Croatia, had popped in to an internet café to catch up on the news and to report progress. While she was there, some virus that was dormant on the machine had stirred and helped itself to her contacts, believing that they were all young rich men in their early twenties in need of transport.

And then emails began to arrive in my inbox from concerned friends and constituents.

Had my wife taken up employment as a sales representative in the automotive industry? Why could she not spell "digital" correctly?

(One sentence in the offending script said "I bought a deigital camera from the website and I got it without one week.")

Corrective action has, we hope, been taken. Her account has been dosed with the digital equivalent of tamiflu and the virus purged. To those constituents who have gone out and bought, on her recommendation, a Kawasaki ZZR for £9500, I say drive carefully. I read it has "a heady maximum of 200hp and is a machine that is used to eating comfortably vast distances. With its stunnin low and mid range torque this iconic bike is practical and virile."

And to the rest of you, I apologise. But of course it wasn't really my fault.

***

A Budget made in Heaven

December 2009

There was a good turn out in the Kingdom of Heaven, as they waited for the Pre Budget Report. The Archangels' bench was packed – they had put in prayer cards to reserve their seats – and many of the cherubs were sitting in the aisles. Some of them were twittering, hoping they wouldn't be noticed by the Speaker. The Gallery was packed with scribes who had to file their epistles before evensong. (They had learned not to believe everything they had been told by the prophets that morning. The Book of Numbers, chiselled in its distinctive pink stone, had been particularly gloomy.)

Then the Keeper of the Holy Purse rose to make his statement, putting his papyrus on a pile of bibles so he could read without using his glasses. "I want to begin by telling you" he said "that we have been living beyond our means. You may all think that we can live up here on the never-never, but I have to tell you in all honesty that that is not the case. All the milk and honey has to be paid for with hard-earned foreign currency. The celestial crown has been losing its value against the pluto, and with the spread of atheism in our dominions, there has been less investment in our stock of undated Peace Loan. I am going to have to announce some tough policies to balance the tablets. We can no longer live on a wing and a prayer."

There was some muttering from the backbenches at this point. They were familiar with the economic cycle whereby seven fat years are followed by seven lean ones but, frankly, they thought they had put that and all the locusts behind them when they reached the Kingdom of Heaven. An end to boom and bust. What had been the point of following Moses and his ten commandments if heaven was going to be just like earth? Leviticus was overheard saying to Ezekiel that they might as well have coveted their neighbour's ox - not to mention his maidservant - after all.

The Keeper of the Holy Purse outlined the options he had explored. Abolition of the Death Grant would save no money as there had been no claims. Investment in the arts – particularly music and choirs - was a manifesto commitment and therefore sacred. "I have, however, been looking at the size of some of our angels and I believe there is scope for some economy in the budget for entertainment and hospitality. A little girdle tightening would not come amiss."

He could not rule out an increase in taxes "I am afraid there may have to be a lot more rendering next year. The current rate of 200 shekels in the talent may have to be reviewed. Our policy is of course to tax things that are bad and this brings me to climate change. Up here above the clouds, we are of course concerned about CO_2 emissions. Our rivals in the afterlife business - and we operate in a competitive global market - have paid the penalty of ignoring scientific advice, and I understand the temperature down there is very uncomfortable. I am minded to convene a summit of all interested parties – though I know what the good book says about supping with the...."

At that point in his address, there was a thunderbolt and darkness fell. The Speaker could be heard talking about a higher authority and announced the suspension of proceedings.

The Smoking Ban

January 2010

Under the 30 year rule, we are now entitled to read the unexpurgated history of the first Thatcher Administration, elected in 1979. Its inner wirings have been laid bare as minutes of meetings, together with her dismissive comments on official submissions, come into the public domain. We read of her impatience with civil servants and Ministers at the lack of radical action to reduce the financial deficit and the numbers in the public sector.

Somewhere in the same archives are recorded the actions of those of us lower down the ministerial food chain who started working the same day. As a Parliamentary-Under Secretary of State, they came no lower. My job was to sign the letters, reply to the late night Adjournment Debates in the House of Commons, meet visiting Ministers of the same lowly rank from overseas, get the Department's legislative programme through the House and, in the words of W S Gilbert, " to run on little errands for the Minister of State." And to appear on the Today Programme when a sacrificial lamb was required.

I arrived at Alexander Fleming House, the Headquarters of what was at that time the Department of Health and Social Security, on the Monday after the election. The foyer was full of smoke, and behind the reception desk was a chain-smoking commissionaire. Not, I thought, a great advertisement for my new policies on preventive medicine. After meeting those who were to work for me in the Private Office, I made some enquiries to see whether we might find, from the army of people the Prime Minister was criticising me for employing, a non-smoker to greet our guests.

My enquiry was made before the first edition of Yes Minister had been screened, so I was an innocent about the machinations of the British Civil Service. A detailed paper was at the top of my red box that very night. My request was of course being taken seriously, and the Department was aware of its responsibilities to promote a non-smoking environment. The zeal of the newly-arrived Parliamentary Under-Secretary of State on the evils of tobacco had been noted from his trenchant speeches as a backbencher in the Parliament that had just ended, when he had criticised the Department's limp-wristed actions. However, the Department was also conscious of its obligations as an employer and it had to respect the contracts of employment with its staff. Legal advice had been taken on my request. (Always a bad sign, as I was to learn later.)

The individual concerned was a popular employee and deeply committed to his work. There had been no complaints about him. There was nothing in his contract of employment that prevented him from smoking while on duty. His Union, the National Union of Public Employees, would take a lively interest in his case if Ministers were minded to move him, against his wishes, to another role. Would it be wise to discuss the matter with the Secretary of State before I took the matter further? (Another bad sign.)

I will never know the outcome of my initiative. Margaret Thatcher moved me from my job before I moved the smoker from his.

***

Going to the Country

January 2010

The man reading Sporting Life over a pint of Guinness in the White Hart had been looking at me out of the corner of his eye, and, as I was about to leave the pub, he sidled over.

"Excuse me – aren't you that MP fella?" I pleaded guilty as charged, and thought about owning up to membership of the Shadow Cabinet as well, so he could consider all my offences at the same time, before pronouncing sentence.

"I want to know when Gordon's going to call the election." he told me. I said I had more than a passing interest in the answer to the question - which my agent kept on asking - and said it would probably be in May. I added quickly that my fleet-footed troops were ready to go at any time (in case he was a spy from an enemy camp).

"Why won't he go in February?" "Not a great month for canvassing" I replied looking at the snow outside, "and he is unlikely to make up the lost ground between now and then. Ted Heath tried it in February and came unstuck. Besides, Gordon didn't go early when he was ahead in 2007, so why should he go early in 2010 when he's behind?"

For reasons that were not clear, he consulted Sporting Life before asking "What about March?" "A possibility" I replied. "But he has said there is going to be a Budget, and that cannot be until after March 9th. That doesn't leave much time to dissolve and have an election before the end of the month."

"What about April?" "Could be messy" I replied "We have local elections on May 6th – and Easter in the middle. You would have two campaigns going on at the same time. A nightmare for election expenses and the agents."

"And June?" "Yes, that would be right up against the buffers. But coming after the local elections on May 6th, there is a risk of voter fatigue. And if he does badly in the locals, that's not a great springboard for the general."

After this lengthy psephological exchange about polling day, I thought I might risk sounding him out about his own intentions.

"Will you be influencing the outcome of this election, whatever the date on which it is held?" I asked cautiously

He looked at me scornfully. "Hell no, I won't be wasting my time by voting – you lot are all the same"

"Why then" I asked "this healthy interest in the date of the poll?"

"I'm thinking of having a bet on the date with Paddy Power. I can get 12 to 1 against April, whereas May is 4 to 1 on."

The Civil Service

February 2010

The phone went at 5.45. 5.45 in the morning. It was the Today Programme, anxious that I should come on air to address that half of the nation that tunes into Radio 4 about whatever subject happened to be the controversy of the day. I was unable to help them straightway, as I was heading for Andover Station to catch the 6.26. This was so I could get to London to address the other half of the nation, which tunes in to Radio 5 Live, on the very same issue.

I did however call the Today Programme from the London bound platform at Andover Station and pre-recorded an interview, which I thought went quite well. Half an hour later, they told me that the quality of the sound had made the interview unusable. The voice of the station announcer telling us that the nine coach train from Salisbury would be arriving shortly and we should not leave our baggage unattended had detracted from the bullet points of my message. If I wanted to address half the nation, I would need to come into their studios, after I had done another programme whose existence they barely acknowledged.

The second interview did not go quite so well. In the interval, while I had been reading the Times on the train and doing the crossword, my interrogator had analysed and dissected my arguments. The coach of a serious football team will video-record his opponents for the next round, and then play and replay their key moves to identify a counter-strategy. This approach had been adopted at Broadcasting House. Or, to switch analogies to chess, the Young Opening Gambit had been scrutinised and opportunities for a serious counter-attack identified.

The moral is to deny the broadcaster a second opportunity, and oblige him to use the original, whatever the sound quality. But there was some better news during the week. At a seminar held by the

Institute for Government, we heard about transitional issues relevant to the forthcoming General Election.

Those who had been around in 1997, when the Blair Government took over from the Major Government, told us how the Civil Service had coped. Lessons had been learned which might be of value later in the year, if there was another change of administration. We were told how important it was for the Shadow Cabinet to contact Permanent Secretaries and share with them their party's aspirations and policies for government. At the end, a civil servant took me into his confidence. As a result of the exchanges between Shadow Cabinet and Permanent Secretaries, and Seminars such as this one, he had a good idea of what would be required of the Civil Service, should my Party win.

What might happen if this Labour Government got back, he told me, was a closed book.

Part 4

(In David Cameron's Cabinet)

A Doorstep Encounter

May 2010

Pleasing one's electorate during a General Election Campaign is difficult, as I have discovered over the past four weeks. For every person whom I propositioned in the privacy of their home who did not want to engage with me, there was an email from another, complaining that I had not canvassed their opinion. Accusations of unwarranted intrusion were countered by those of indolent complacency. Before the next election, which we had all hoped might be four years away but could now be closer, I need a system that identifies those who want to meet their Conservative candidate; and those who would be more likely to vote for him if the encounter did not take place.

I did meet a huge number of people, most of whom were courteous and 58.4% of whom voted for me. A sincere vote of thanks to them.

One wavering voter I met told me he was doing a doctoral thesis on the role of logic in the English language. Memories of A J Ayer's seminal work "Language, Truth and Logic", which I had read 50 years ago, swam before my eyes. "Logic and mathematics are true, simply because we never allow them to be anything else", I recalled the Professor saying. The voter was impressed with this when I tried it out on him, so I moved on to David Hume's theory that it was never possible to deduce judgements of value from matters of fact. The lady who was accompanying me, holding the leaflets and the canvass cards, began to exhibit signs of impatience at this philosophical exchange, so we moved on to the telephone conversation with my philosophy tutor at Oxford – a man who wouldn't use one word if none would do.

I telephoned him once to let him know I could not attend my tutorial with him. This was in the days when one had to put coins into the box in the telephone – the more the coins, the longer the call. As I fumbled with the coins, I heard his instructions to the caller "Put in threepence, sixpence or a shilling. Preferably threepence."

The time came to bring the discussion with the voter to a conclusion. "That was very interesting" I said – "But how will you be voting on Thursday?" There was a pause while he reflected on what I had said. "That is not the right question. You know perfectly well how I will vote. I will go into the polling station, be given a ballot paper and mark it with a cross. The question you should have asked was "For whom will you be voting?" I marked him down as a "Don't Know" and moved on.

In the weekend after past General Elections when my Party has done well, I have sat by the telephone waiting to hear if my services were required by my Leader. Sometimes the phone rang and sometimes it didn't. This time, I have sat by the television, waiting to find out who won the election.

***

Changes to your Account

June 2010

We politicians are meant to be silver-tongued. We sell you dreams and promise to make them come true. We spin and weave. You can turn on the radio in the morning, tune in to the Today Programme and hear us at work. We speak of responding to the challenges of climate change and global recession, rather than putting up fuel prices and cutting public expenditure.

Ministers speak not of tax rises but of fiscal tightening. Putting up interest rates is called monetary discipline. Devaluation is the realignment of currencies. Cuts are efficiency measures. I make no partisan point here – we politicians all speak the same language.

But we have met our match. I have a letter from the company who keeps my Blackberry connected to the outside world. On an hourly basis, it informs me of my Party's Line to Take, and warns me of the dangers of responding to questionnaires.

The letter from my service provider started off innocuously enough. "We're writing to update you about some changes to your Business Account."

The average punter in the street might not have been alarmed by this. But we politicians recognise doublespeak when we see it.

There followed a paragraph designed to lower suspicions "From August 2010 onwards, we will be operating a new Online Billing system."

Fine, many utilities now do this, and the company set out in some detail the benefits of the new regime. Access 24 hours a day to my account, and "visibility of the most up-to-date status." No problem.

Then followed some good news for Friends of the Earth. This change would reduce the amount of paper, and enable me to pass on to children and grandchildren a world full of trees.

And then, when one's resistance had been lowered, the kick in the teeth. "Registering for this online service will also ensure that you avoid a £1.25 monthly charge for paper invoices." So the "updating of the changes to my account" was in fact a threatened price increase. Insult was then added to injury, with their proposals for direct debits.

"Another incentive for switching to direct debit is that you'll avoid having to pay an administration charge of £5 that will be applied from July."

So my service provider is going to reduce his costs – or, more correctly, I am going to reduce his costs for him. And, if I don't, he will increase mine.

It is decision time, and I am drafting a letter to my service provider telling him that I am withdrawing my custom. It begins, appropriately "I am writing to update you about some changes to my Business Account with you."

A Cliffhanger

August 2010

Our holiday ended a fortnight ago, and readers will be relieved to hear that our luggage sailed through all the tests devised to keep it off the plane, without payment of a substantial premium. As indeed did its owners, who presented themselves well before the prescribed time before take-off, with the appropriate documentation. We encountered no stag parties, no air rage and no industrial disputes.

We spent a week in Salzburg soaking up culture. Many go there to pay homage to the Von Trapp family, but the music whose sound we were after was Mozart's and his contemporaries. On our way to the Opera House, we went through the Mirabell Gardens, where Maria von Trapp and the children had danced around the statue of Pegasus singing "Do re mi". The songs we were due to hear were vocally more challenging, though less intelligible as they would be sung in a foreign tongue.

One performance had us on the edge of our seats and it was excellent - but not for the reason you expect.

We had bought tickets to hear Matthias Göerne sing Schubert's song-cycle – Die Schöne Müllerin – with Christopher Eschenbach at the keyboard. This tells the tale of the apprentice looking for work, and falling in love with the Miller's daughter. It ends in tragedy, with suicide in a brook after his advances are rejected because the Miller's daughter prefers the hunter.

The singer we were listening to emoted as he sang, communicating with his body language the moods of the lover. He lent forwards, and he lent backwards; he lowered himself and he stood on his toes, usually when Schubert had prescribed one of the higher notes in the baritone range.

He did all this close to the Steinway grand piano, on which Mr Eschenbach was heavily engaged. Matthias' right hand rested on top of the piano.

The problem arose when two movements happened simultaneously; the leaning backwards, and the standing on his toes. (He could do this while remaining vertical, because one foot was placed in front of the other) This was because the open lid of the piano, held in place by a piece of wood, was inches behind his head. We could see this, but he couldn't. When these movements were combined, he risked raising by an inch or two the lid of the piano. Of itself, this might not have mattered. But had he done so, the stick that held up the lid would have been released. The lid would have come down, like the bonnet of a car. His right hand would have been pulped. The resulting cry of anguish would have been one that Schubert would have found difficult to score.

Each time the head moved dangerously close to the lid, the audience held its breath. Some moved forwards in their seat, hoping to encourage the singer also to move forward. The eyebrows of the accompanist implied that he was not unaware of the potential drama, as he busily depicted the babbling of the brook on the keyboard, asking himself if his first aid skills would be adequate.

But unlike the tale of the apprentice, this one ended happily with the singer in one piece. As far as we know. The two of them were due to do the sequel – Die Winterreise – a few days later. But I couldn't go through that all over again, so we went to see the Salzburg puppets doing the Sound of Music.

***

Credit Card

November 2010

I have some sympathy with those countries that are having liquidity problems. Lines of credit disappear; current consumption is curtailed and the gold reserves are used to pay for food. My sympathy is based on the recent cancellation of the Young credit card, which has reproduced these problems on a smaller scale. (One of the cards disappeared and so the account had to be stopped). Purchases then had to be restricted to what could be bought with the cash in hand until triple A rating was restored.

The day after the card disappeared, I rang up the company and asked for a replacement. No problem; it would be despatched to me shortly. An email then arrived from the contractor entrusted with the delivery, asking me to be at my home, equipped with my passport, for a substantial chunk of a working day. The card was registered at my London address and I am not there during the working day. If I was, the Whips and my constituents would want to know why.

So I asked for it to be delivered to my home in Hampshire, where my wife would be standing at the door, like Penelope waiting for Ulysses, with my passport in one hand and a pen to sign for the card in the other. There was a period of e-silence. Then the bad news; credit cards cannot be sent to a second residential address.

This was the time for lateral thinking. As a good Tory, I thought about competition, choice and the magic of the market-place. My credit card had come from a well-known supermarket chain with at least one branch in Andover. There is another chain, also with more than one branch in Andover, who supply credit cards as well as food and who might have a more liberal policy on card delivery.

I went online to apply for one. My credit rating should be reasonable. I have had the same job for 39 years and, if the Fixed Term Parliament Bill goes through, I will have it for another 4 years, 5 months and nine days. I have lived in the same place for 13 years, and there are no county court orders outstanding or local creditors petitioning for bankruptcy. The salary of an MP, in the public domain, is three times the national average. I sent the form off and, within seconds, the reply came back.

During this time, I was told, my application had been given careful consideration. But, on this occasion, the decision was not to extend to me the opportunity of having one of their credit cards. No adverse conclusions should be drawn from this decision, said the email – though it was difficult to see the silver lining in the cloud.

As I reflected on my misfortune of not getting one card because I owned two homes and not getting the other because a computer had decided I couldn't afford either, the post arrived.

Without the need to produce any document, Supermarket No. 1 had sent the replacement cards. We leapt into the car and drove off to buy some food before they changed their mind.

***

Annie's Bar

January 2011

Before Christmas, as Leader of the House at Business Questions, I was asked to find time for a debate in the Commons on the future of the horse racing levy. For those unfamiliar with the turf, this is a statutory levy on the horseracing business of bookmakers and the Tote, which is then distributed to improve matters equestrian and to advance veterinary science. While horses in North West Hampshire cannot vote, their welfare is of political importance. The Balding clan in Kingsclere and Kimpton generate jobs and trophies, as do other trainers and breeders. And of course we have betting shops a-plenty. I had much sympathy with the request for a debate and was delighted that the Backbench Business Committee found time for one during the month.

While there is legitimate interest in betting in the House, gambling on the premises is discouraged. There is a Bridge Team, for the more cerebral members of both Houses, but I am assured they do not play for money. Sporting Life can be found in the tea-room with circles ringed round certain fancied runners; colleagues may own all or parts of a racehorse or greyhound; some are spotted at racecourses around the country; but the conspicuous placing of bets in Parliament is, as I say, frowned on.

But there have in the past been ventures that sailed quite close to the wind. In the 1970s, a group of Members would meet before lunch in Annie's Bar and pour over a puzzle on the back page of one of the daily papers. The puzzle would comprise ten jumbled up letters, and the challenge was to find as many words of three or more letters as possible; and, crucially, the 10 letter word that used all the letters once. The word would be, for example, hypsometer, proscenium or narcolepsy. That was round one, which produced a sharp-witted winner, familiar with crossword puzzles and anagrams.

Round 2 involved less intellectual energy, but a lot more nerve and imagination. Round 2 was won by the MP who mentioned that word first in parliamentary proceedings later in the day and got it into Hansard (the Official Record). This meant looking at the Order Paper and finding some proceeding in the Chamber or in Committee which related to the subject; concocting a speech which was both relevant to the subject of debate and contained the key word; catching the Speaker's eye and delivering the speech without being ruled out of order.

Along with Annie's Bar, the competition came to an end a few decades ago. No money changed hands; but the winner didn't have to buy a round for a day or two.

***

A Flutter on the National

April 2011

I am not a regular visitor to the country's betting shops. I go there at election times – not to bet on myself, as that would be insider trading – but to assist those colleagues fighting challenging seats elsewhere in the country.

The tactic is simple. On a whistle-stop tour of enemy territory, my task is to get the picture of the Conservative candidate in the local paper; to convey infectious optimism about his or her prospects; and to drum up business for local traders.

These three targets can be hit simultaneously by marching into the local betting shop with the candidate, and asking what the odds are on him or her winning the seat. There is a pause, as it is usually a question that no one has asked before. Someone in the back office interrogates a computer or, on occasions, rings up the editor of the local paper. I am then told that he or she is 50 to 1. "A bargain!" I cry, producing a five pound note from my wallet. The cameras snap me and the candidate, wearing our blue rosettes, as the betting slip changes hands; the bookmaker is enriched by £5; and I get a betting ticket of unknown value to add to my collection. The news that a Senior Politician has placed this bet on an outsider reverberates around the punting world and the odds are slashed to 25 to 1.

It is a sad fact that I have never returned to collect my winnings – perhaps as well, as the bets are placed with local bookmakers many miles away in Wales or Scotland. But I have secured more publicity than a £5 advertisement would ever have bought.

However, I did have a flutter on the Grand National last week. We did some careful research on form and then decided to back a horse that had the same name as a grandson. I took time off from the Advice Bureau last Saturday to pop into Jenningsbet in the High Street and put £5 each way on Oscar Time. My ticket tells me that I was served by Kevin at 9.32.36 (GMT) on Till 007202. My maximum potential return was £85.

Further research revealed that was also a horse called George running and we considered hedging our bets. But two visits to a betting shop in one day would have looked addictive.

We settled down over a cup of tea to watch the race. With Oscar Time well placed behind the leader's shoulder as they came up to the final hurdle, it looked as if we would be seeing a little more of Kevin and the contents of Till 007202. But Oscar ran out of puff and came second.

Still, it was an each way bet and the winnings will keep the goldfinches in Niger seed for two weeks.

The Referendum

May 2011

Elections are not quite the same if one is not a candidate. One's own future is not on the line, so there is less adrenaline in the system. But, as the local councillors were good enough to turn out last year to drum up support for me, I owed it to them to return the favour. And of course I have an interest in maintaining, nay expanding, local support for my Party. Which, I am happy to say, is what happened.

After knocking on one door I was asked by a perceptive constituent whether I was standing for Test Valley Borough Council myself. "No" I replied "I am calling on behalf of my very good and hard-working friends..." Before I could recite the names of the three candidates, I was interrupted. "Why are you wearing a rosette that says 'We're Keeping Young'?"

A good question. To which the answer was that blue rosettes are a scarce commodity, rationed out by the Agent. This was a trophy from last year's General Election. Or, possibly, from any of the previous nine as it is a slogan that has worn well, even if its promoter has not.

Continuing my canvassing session in Augusta Park was a challenge. Some of the development is so new that there are no street signs; and some of the houses are so recently built that there are no numbers.

Obeying instructions from Headquarters, I sought to engage my constituents in the constitutional issue of the Referendum on the Alternative Vote, held on the same day as the local elections. I accosted a man in a string vest who was washing his car. Reluctantly he paused and approached me, a bouquet of body odour surrounding him. Menacingly, he held a dirty sponge in his right hand and a running hose in his left. "Will you be voting No in the Referendum on Thursday?" I asked. He thought about this. "Would that make it easier to get rid of you, George?" he replied defiantly. "Probably not," I replied. "Anyone getting over 50% of the votes in the first round is elected – last time I got 58%." His face fell. The hose twitched and he tightened his grip on the sponge as if to say there were alternative routes to his destination. "Would AV make you work harder and be more honest?" He had obviously read the "Yes to AV" leaflet with its surprising assertion that if politicians were elected by a different system, this would recalibrate their integrity. "No." I replied. His finger lingered over the tip of the hose, increasing the muzzle velocity of the waterflow.

"No bloody point in it then" he concluded and returned to the task in hand. And, to judge from the result, he spoke for the nation.

***

Premium Bonds

June 2011

Much of the work of the local MP is spent unravelling the knots of the bureaucratic system that entangle our constituents. We are broadly familiar with tapers, capital disregards, deferred benefits, non-dependent deductions, passported entitlements, work capacity assessments and the rest of the language spoken by those with A level Benefit Speak.

But every now and then, we have our own difficulties to address. For we too interface with Government Departments; and, when we do, we empathise with our constituents. Or, to put it more aptly, we bond with them.

Many years ago, when the children were small, they acquired a handful of Premium Bonds. Their godparents had deemed it prudent to reduce the National Debt – at that time a fraction of what it is now – by investing in National Savings and having a modest flutter on behalf of the young Youngs.

Ernie never smiled on these bonds and, frankly, I had forgotten about them. Going through some old files, I came across them. They asserted that they had been issued under Section 12 of the National Loans Act 1968 and were non-transferable. On the back, the bond states it "is of no value to anyone but the registered holder."

Which brings me to the point. Each bond is indeed of no value to three of our four children; but, by a process of elimination, it is of value to one of them. But the bonds had no indication of whom they belonged to – an oversight for which I plead guilty. I knew they were not registered in my name nor indeed in that of my wife.

Anxious to reunite the bonds with their rightful owners, I wrote to NSandI in Glasgow to see who they belonged to.

Readers who are fans of Gilbert and Sullivan will know that one of the two gondoliers in the Savoy Opera of that name is the King of Barataria, but no one knew which. Until an old nanny was found who held the answer. NSandI in Glasgow would play the role of Inez, the nurse of the infant King of Barataria, and reveal all.

I typed out the numbers of the bonds; explained that they were not mine but my children's; and asked if they would let me know which bonds belonged to which child.

There was a small delay and I got a terse reply. The Data Protection Act had kicked in; or possibly the Freedom of Information Act; or Section 13 of the National Loans Act 1968; or, again, the Money Laundering legislation. NSandI were unable to tell me more than that which I already knew - the bonds were not registered in my name. Full stop.

Suggestions on a postcard please.

A Birthday Present

July 2011

One of the disadvantages of holding high office is that one's birthday is publicised in the quality press. However, compared with some of the things they print about politicians today, perhaps one should not complain about this minor exposure. This year, my birthday was of biblical significance and generated more interest; I am grateful to constituents for their good wishes – from supporters and opponents alike.

Our children were determined that the event should be appropriately celebrated and they did some research. They discovered that, 50 years ago, I was the proud owner of a red Austin Healey, registration FPH 49. For younger readers, I should explain that this was a high-powered two-seater sports car. It was a car I was very fond of, owning it while pursuing my future wife at Oxford and neglecting my academic studies.   After we got married, it had to go to make way for more conventional transport, capable of accommodating a growing family. My two-seated days were behind me.

Last weekend, there was a throaty roar outside the front door and a crunch of gravel. Outside our home was a red Austin Healey with the appropriate registration. This, I was informed, was a birthday present from the children. I was lost for words. These vehicles are now worth serious money, and while the next generation of Youngs are doing well, I doubted whether they could really afford this extravagance.

They couldn't. What they had done was to hire the car for two days, so I could drive to the family home for a birthday party and then drive back. And very nostalgic it was, bowling along the M4 with the wind blowing through what was left of my hair, our posteriors but a few inches above the tarmac.

When we got to the party, my wife and I were no longer on speaking terms. Not because the magic had gone out of the marriage, but because the noise of the car rendered all conversation impossible. The decibel count from the engine was like a pneumatic drill, amplified by the rattling of the arthritic joints of the car.

One takes for granted the advance of technology; brakes that stop you promptly; power-assisted steering; cars that start first time without the choke.

For example, the fuel gauge was binary. It showed the tank as either full or empty. For 100 miles it was full; then I went up a hill and it was empty. Going down the other side it reverted to full again. After 150 miles it oscillated wildly. These things matter, because the fuel it consumes is not sold at every garage. The long forgotten skill of double-declutching to change gear had to be resurrected, together with hand signals.

After two days, the car was returned to its owner. A moment of youth had been recaptured and old memories revived. But it was a relief to get back into the family saloon, switch on the radio and relapse into anonymity on the A303.

Any Questions? (1)

July 2011

There are two sorts of questions in my life as a Member of Parliament. Business and Any.

Business Questions occur once a week when the House of Commons is sitting. (11.30 on a Thursday morning on the Parliament Channel, if you have nothing better to do.) To the extent that any politician answers a question, I answer them on my own as Leader of the House. As long as the questioner asks for a debate on the subject, he or she can ask about anything. Diseases I have never heard of, places I have never been to, sports I have never played, food I have never eaten, celebrities I have never met. Average playing time, about 50 minutes.

Any Questions also occurs weekly, but my participation is much less frequent. It has certain similarities in that it also lasts about 50 minutes, a time to which my ability to concentrate has now been stretched. But it has crucial differences. Questions are answered, but the duty is shared with three other people who have been selected by the BBC to give different answers. The questions tend to be about topical issues I have heard of, not least to retain the programme's audience. It is presided over by a Dimbleby without a tie and gown, instead of a Speaker with both. And more people tune in.

A fortnight ago, just when I was looking forward to six weeks with no Business Questions because of the Summer Recess, I was summoned to the RAF Museum in Hendon to do Any Questions. This is a gentler version than BBC 1's Question Time, where politicians are eaten alive. Any Questions on Radio 4 is attended by herbivores not carnivores. Dimbleby Minor and the panel weaved their way through World War II aircraft suspended from the ceiling to a hall to answer their questions.

There are usually two right of centre politicians on the panel and two left of centre politicians. The answers to the first question on the Government's approach to growth was therefore a disappointment. I defended the Government's policies, and the two left of centre chaps, on cue, attacked it. The chair then invited my fellow centre-right panellist, whom I had not met before, to share her views. Unsportingly, she allied herself with the other side and I felt like taking off in a Spitfire.

I shared the platform with another ex-Transport Secretary and correctly anticipated that there would be a transport related question. This gave me the opportunity for the soundbite I had been waiting to deliver.

"You wait ages for a Transport Secretary, and then two of them come along at once." The herbivores loved it. None of my other replies evoked the same spontaneous applause. I might try it in the House.

***

Jane Austen

November 2011

And so, to an undisclosed location in the constituency, to find the home of my grandfather's grandmother's aunt, one Jane Austen. Fanny Catherine Knight was Jane Austen's favourite niece, and she married Sir Edward Knatchbull, a Member of Parliament for Kent. Such abilities as I may have both to write and to represent people in the House of Commons may be traced back to this union and the combination of literary and political genes that came with it, via my maternal great-grandfather.

On their engagement, Fanny wrote to her friend "If you have heard that I am engaged to be married to Sir Edward Knatchbull, I am now writing to confirm that intelligence and I need not add that it gives my family the greatest satisfaction, and that with a man of his excellence of character my prospect of as much comfort as this world can bestow is well-founded and I trust not unreasonable." This strikes me as a somewhat self-centred and unromantic response to the baronet's proposal of marriage; indeed, Sir Edward was more emotional about the engagement. He wrote to her "Allow me to say that you are the only person in whose Society I can find Happiness," adding as an afterthought " and to whose example and care I could entrust the welfare of my children."

Sir Edward was on the right side of the debate on slavery – he was against it; and on the wrong side of the debate on the Great Reform Bill. He was against that as well. But he represented the good folk of Kent for many years, at times being elected unopposed. One of the last entries in his diaries dated September 28th 1846 has a familiar ring to it "..the state of the whole of Europe, the condition of England – its dense population, its large national debt, the want of sufficient employment - the dissatisfaction openly avowed and secretly entertained, the loss of confidence in public men...may make the boldest heart to tremble." Indeed, that was exactly what happened to that organ, for he expired shortly after.

But I digress. On arrival at the site of the Rectory where Jane's father had lived, I met the volunteers excavating the foundations, under the benign guidance of the Heritage Lottery Fund who are paying for the work. I asked what they had discovered about the lifestyle of my ancestors, and was told that they smoked and drank a lot. The evidence was compelling; mounds of clay pipes, and many empty wine bottles. The care being taken was impressive – like detectives at a scene of crime. Minute particles were examined and, if of interest, put in a plastic bag and labelled. A local resident with a metal detector then went through the discarded soil to see if anything had been missed.

A representative of the Jane Austen Society was on the site and I introduced myself as the local MP and a descendant of the Rector whose lifestyle was being exposed. This intelligence cut no ice. I was instead rebuked for being a non-member of the Society. An application form to join has just arrived in the post.

The Ancient Euro

November 2011

People may think that the problems that beset the leaders of the eurozone countries today are the product of the sophisticated world in which we live, when information is transmitted at the touch of a button, and people can travel across national boundaries with ease. But I can reveal that the same difficult choices, though on a more modest scale, confronted folk in Andover thousands of years ago.

The small settlement was dominated by four families, each with a head of household. One was a farmer, one a builder, one a weaver and the last was a priest. Between them, they provided the material and spiritual needs of the community. They appreciated, long before today's economists had put a name to it, the benefits of the division of labour. If the farmer didn't have to build and maintain stone and wooden dwellings, or make clothes for his family but spent his time farming, his output could be maximised to the value of the community as a whole. And likewise with the rest of them.

To achieve this desired outcome, they needed a measurement of the value of what they produced – a common currency. They met to resolve this thorny issue and with the help of a prayer from the priest and a beverage brewed for the occasion by the farmer, engaged in serious discussion. They soon reached agreement on the value of the output of the farmer, the builder and the weaver, but had problems valuing the output of the priest. The priest asserted that eternal happiness in the life hereafter was worth more than the creature comforts of this transient world and therefore worth far more than a year's supply of corn and dead rabbits; a lifetime's supply of altar cloths and surplices; or an extension to the rectory. But the farmer was an atheist, arguing that, if the priest was any good at his job, there would not have been a series of poor harvests. After another round of Andover special brew, they reached agreement on a pricing mechanism, without needing to resort to qualified majority voting or a local referendum.

And off they went. The farmer farmed, the builder built, the weaver wove and the priest prayed. The priest, being the best educated of the four, had been given the task of keeping the accounts. The time came for the first Annual General Meeting at which it became clear, without the intervention of the Court of Auditors, that the weaver owed a large sum of money – in fact over 100% of his gross national output. The farmer, who had done quite well out of the agricultural policy and had produced a small butter mountain, argued that the weaver took long holidays, knocked off while it was still light and had been able to acquire a large coracle which he kept on the River Anton. The priest was prepared to offer the weaver forgiveness, both spiritual and material, but the others objected to any write-off of the debt. They demanded that the weaver be expelled from the common currency zone.

Sounds familiar?

***

A Letter to Santa

December 2011

The following missive was sent to Father Christmas' Private Secretary by the Head of Legal Services at Father Christmas Inc.

"Forgive a late submission, but with a highly seasonal business such as this one, my Department is exceptionally busy at this time of year; and we have also had to tighten our belts during the recession. There are a number of issues on which I need to update FC.

We have disposed of the cases from 2010 alleging mis-selling, which were up from the previous year. The Office of Fair Trading have told those whose requests were not granted that FC cannot be held responsible for claims made by non-accredited agents. Some of those who brought cases were deemed too young to prosecute in their own right, and their parents, who were liable to be cited by us as co-defendants, did not want the matter pursued. We have also re-imbursed Royal Mail for a large number of items sent with inadequate postage, and settled out of court one charge of driving a sleigh without due care and attention.

Turning to this year, we have had a number of allegations of child molestation in department stores during the run-up to Christmas. We have disposed of these by referring to the large number of impersonators who are around - our Patent Licence still has not been approved, although it was applied for in 1886. The Criminal Records Bureau remain content with your nil entry and remind you that, to safeguard your own reputation, you should never be alone with a child under 10.

There has been an outbreak of brucellosis on the Arabian Peninsular; any reindeer that have been there will not be admitted to European Union countries. We have had to make alternative arrangements for delivery to the Middle East. Otherwise our reindeer will be impounded by EU vets and kept under supervision for several weeks at our expense. Our insurers are not prepared to take this risk.

We have secured the necessary clearances for our operations on December 24th and 25th from International Air Traffic Control and this year there is, unusually, no reported industrial action.

Finally, I need to update you on the case before the European Court of Human Rights. As you know, the case against Father Christmas is scheduled for a hearing on the grounds of discrimination against women. The assertion is that, before children are old enough to be able to come to an independent judgement, they are led to believe that the qualities of generosity and good humour with which Father Christmas is traditionally associated may encourage the view that those qualities are not equally present in mothers. The case, brought by Mothers for Justice, is however unlikely to be heard before the ECHR has dealt with a case which raises similar issues of gender discrimination – that against Lord God Almighty."

Up in the Gods

January 2012

With my presence not required in the House one evening last month, a quick surf on the cultural internet showed that Verdi's La Traviata was on at the Royal Opera House. Further research revealed that two tickets were left for this popular production - one at £180 and the other at £9.

There were a number of reasons for this wide disparity, distance from the stage being one and height above sea level being another. More important, the £9 was not a ticket for a seat. It was a licence to rent for the evening a square foot of carpet on which a slimline tenant would stand while Violetta, whose problems were admittedly more severe than mine, would sing until her demise from consumption in Act 3.

Recalling my time as a student of economics, I drew an indifference curve to resolve the dilemma of whether to go, and if so, where to go. Price was on the horizontal axis. Enthusiasm for La Traviata on the y axis, then moderated by a factor for comfort. The intersection was closer to £9 than £0. So a purchase was indicated. And the intersection was a lot closer to £9 than £180. By the time this calculation had been done, the expensive ticket had been bought by someone with a deeper pocket or thicker waistline, so I reserved the last ticket and cycled off for some culture. (Had the opera been one of Wagner's marathons, the decision might have been different.)

The ticket may have been at the bottom of the range, but this was compensated for by the height of the viewing platform. What were surtitles for the rest of the audience were subtitles for us in the Upper Amphitheatre. We were warned that those who suffered from vertigo should not invest. I looked up to see where the oxygen masks might drop down from and defended my Lebensraum from my neighbour – a large gentleman still getting his breath back from climbing the stairs.

Although the performance was a nominal sell-out, as the lights dimmed it was clear that some of the seats in front of us were unoccupied. And this is what separated the sheep from the goats. As the ushers closed the doors and withdrew, a lithe 25 year old standing two away from me slipped, like a greyhound out of a trap, into an empty seat in front, leaving me and many others twice her age standing for three hours. I will know better next time.

***

Money Laundering

February 2012

Too much debt. That is what we have been told is at the root of many of our problems. Too much Government debt; too much personal debt; too much corporate debt. Economies built on the shaky foundations of irresponsible lending must be replaced by ones underpinned by prudent and sustainable financing. Debt to GDP ratios of over 120% will bring the IMF, the European Central Bank, or the local bank manager to the door with demands for austerity.

If we are able to, we should play a part in reducing indebtedness and an opportunity has presented itself. The Young tribe is not immortal, and, every so often, one of us falls off the perch. Last year, a relative died and legacies filtered through the system, with the Treasury taking its cut. The sum was not large but, crucially, it was more than £5000.

At this point, the imperative to reduce debt meets the imperative to prevent money laundering. I am even more supportive of the need to prevent crooks laundering money than I am of the need to reduce debt. But it was soon to become clear that there was, how shall we put it, some tension between the two.

My letter to the financial institution privileged to lend me money and offering it the opportunity to lend me less was met with the following response.

"You may recall from the Handbook that if debt reduction occurs for this amount (over £5000) then we must comply with Money Laundering Regulations. To assist you in dealing with this procedure, we enclose a response form for your completion and return, attaching any supporting documentary evidence." The Money Laundering Response Form, with fifteen boxes to be completed, made it clear that its author was required to be satisfied that the funds were from a legitimate source and "are not the proceeds of any crime." The Young tribe does not engage in financial crime and I am pretty certain that my late relative led a blameless life. But my assertion would not be enough to satisfy the anti-money launderers. Evidence from solicitors was going to have to be adduced.

There may be solicitors who work for nothing but mine doesn't. The search for evidence and the cost of the relevant correspondence threatens to erode the impact of my debt reduction policy.

And this raises a broader question I leave with readers. When the Greek Government tries to repay the billions of Euros it has just borrowed, will its Prime Minister have to complete a Money Laundering Response Form?

Any Questions? (2)

March 2012

A fortnight ago, I woke up to Radio 4's Today Programme – compulsory listening for the modern politician. Two items caught my attention. The first was "The Coalition Government has just had the worst two weeks in its life." And the second was "Joining our panel on Any Questions tonight is the Leader of the House of Commons, Sir George Young." It was not a good start to my day.

Those close to me contacted me later on to say that it was a sign of confidence in me that I had been chosen to front the case for the administration in such challenging circumstances; but the truth was that I had been offered a choice of slots a month earlier and had plumped for this one, without forecasting that the political heavens were about to open.

There is a silver lining to every cloud. That day the Government was under attack on no less than three issues. (To avoid re-opening old wounds, I will not remind readers what they were.) There was therefore a good chance that each would be the subject of interrogation on Any Questions. Why was this good news? Because it narrowed the subjects on which the panellist would need to be briefed. On a normal Any Questions programme, those defending the Government need to patrol a long frontier, and be ready to repel insurgents at whatever point they might attack. But, as the BBC had announced the areas where it believed the Government to be vulnerable, defences could be reinforced in the appropriate locations.

Later on in the Today Programme, there was some relief. The Labour Party had lost one of its parliamentary strongholds - Bradford West. This was better news for two reasons. First, it ensured that this would be the subject of a fourth question, further eliminating the need for briefing on other news items; and, second, it meant that another member of the panel would be the subject of some light grilling by our host.

The programme ran to form and the two politicians emerged at the end suitably chastened. No amount of training and briefing by our teams could convince the audience that our profession was an honourable one. The two non-politicians on the panel had a walk-over.

But there was consolation at the end of the day. Yes, it was a four hour drive from Otley in Yorkshire back home; but this was the week with wall-to-wall Schubert on Radio 3. It restored the spirits to listen to some of his finest works; and the BBC driver told me he had never listened to so much classical music.

***

The Advice Bureau

May 2012

Before I became an MP, I shadowed a Member of Parliament for a few days, to see if this was how I wanted to spend the rest of my life (assuming a constituency could be found to accommodate this ambition). I watched this hero orate in the Chamber, stroke the party faithful in the constituency, and deal with his Advice Bureau in his Association offices, where he listened patiently to the concerns of his constituents. They were predominantly about income support, or supplementary benefit, as it was known at the time. At the end of each interview, he would ask the constituent to stay while he handwrote a personal letter to the Minister, asking for the grievance to be remedied and the stream of income to be promptly resumed. He would sign the letter with the familiar green portcullis at its top, seal it in an envelope, address it to the Minister and hand it to the constituent with an instruction to pop it in a letter box. "My good friend Paul, the Minister at the Department, has all the answers," he would say, as the constituent was ushered from the room after a handshake.

It was an impressive performance and, when I eventually got into Parliament, I found myself sitting next to Paul in the tea-room. I asked him whether my hero's letters had brought instant relief to his constituents. "Bloody nightmare." Paul replied "No one could read a single word he wrote; we had to ring his secretary to find out what had happened."

With the help of modern technology, could I not achieve the objective of my role model by showing folk the speed of my response? Mindful of the need to keep expenditure down, I purchased on *b*y a second-hand portable printer. As I conduct my Advice Bureau, it sits on the desk, connected by an umbilical cord to the laptop. (The budget did not stretch to blue teeth). After each interview, letters are typed up, printed out and signed. One letter is to Paul's successors as Ministers and the other to the constituent.

The Saturday post in Andover High Street goes at 12.30, and as I popped the letters in the pillar box at 12.25 after the first run of the new regime, I hoped my constituents would be impressed by getting my letter on Monday morning.

There was indeed a response on Monday morning. Royal Mail telephoned to say that I needed to adjust the template on my letters so the address in the window envelope could be read by the postmen. My writing was legible, but sadly invisible.

Moths

July 2012

"Lay not up for yourselves treasures upon earth, where moth and rust doth corrupt, and where thieves break through and steal." Thieves that break through and steal are a hazard we are as familiar with today as was St Matthew when he wrote those words two thousand years ago. We can minimise the risk, in a way his readers couldn't at the time, by placing our denarii and shekels in the bank - a safer bet than the money-changers in the temple (Admittedly thieves can now steal from the bank without the inconvenience of breaking through, thanks to modern technology; but our funds are covered by the deposit guarantee scheme.) The loss of other earthly treasures we can insure against, so long as they are not destroyed by an Act of God, many of which are chronicled elsewhere by Matthew.

But it is the first of the three hazards mentioned by the gospeller that is of most relevance to the Young household today. (Rust is not an issue because the car seems to me to be made mostly of plastic, and the bicycles are kept warm and dry.) The problem is the common clothes moth or *tineola bisselliella,* to give it its Roman name. It is not often that I have to don formal attire, but a series of constitutional and Jubilee-related events stipulating formal dress in May and June necessitated the wearing of the morning coat. This lives a quiet life at one end of the cupboard in my London flat, seeing daylight when I am invited to a smart wedding or to perform a small walk-on part at the State Opening of Parliament. As the coat was removed from the cupboard after winter hibernation, a well-fed specimen of tineola bisselliella flew out. It could have been a largeola bisselliella. Fortunately, its diet had been modest enough not to cause visible damage to the morning coat, but closer inspection of the wardrobe revealed that it was not alone. And that it had cousins that had colonised other edible parts of the flat.

It is a compliment that the moth has chosen my flat as its habitat. Clothes moths live on keratin, which is found in natural fibres such as wool, cashmere and silk. It is the more expensive clothes, I am told, that are targeted by clothes moths. There are two challenges to be confronted. One is to eliminate the moths and their larvae from London; the second is to avoid cross-contamination with the home in the constituency. The diet in my small bachelor pad in Westminster is as nothing compared with the feast available in keratin-rich Hampshire.

***

The Olympics

August 2012

Like thousands of my constituents, I made the pilgrimage to London to watch part of the Olympics. My destination was the Excel Centre, where the judo, table tennis, fencing, wrestling and weightlifting were taking place in five different arenas.

Most of my journey was done by train, but the last section was completed on two wheels, at a more sedate pace than that set by Bradley Wiggins. I wanted to test the Olympic route for its green credentials and I was struck by the lack of other traffic on the road. It was a slight disappointment to find only 12 other bicycles in the bicycle park at the Excel centre, but the truth is that public transport via the Docklands Light Railway took you right to the door.

I watched the final of the Mens' Table Tennis, dominated by the Chinese. I have to report a worrying development in the game, cross-contaminated from its big brother, lawn tennis. Readers may share my annoyance at the screaming or grunting from women tennis players, each time they play a shot. It is my uncharitable view that this is often done with the objective of distracting the opponent, and hence is Unsporting Behaviour. One of the finalists in the Mens' Table Tennis has copied this. As he served, he stamped his foot on the floor very hard. (This is preceded by a ritual. The ball is put in the left hand, which is then sealed over the ball by the right hand. He stoops until his eye is level with the table. The left hand is then raised to eye level, and, as a magician reveals an egg from nowhere, the palm is uncurled flat to reveal the ball. It is then lobbed and served, accompanied by a petulant stamp.) I am happy to report that he lost.

If the promoters of Team GB are looking for a sport in which to invest before Rio where we have not traditionally done well, table tennis is one. The overheads are a fraction of those for cycling, rowing and dressage and I suspect the majority of the population have played the game at some point, so are familiar with the rules.

These have changed since I last played. Then, you won when you reached 21, and you changed service every five points. Now, it is first to 11, and service changes every two points. I was sitting next to the President of the Dutch Table Tennis Federation – a connoisseur of the game – so I asked him why the rules had been changed. The answer came back that the game was taking too long to get to 21. I asked him if he had ever been to a Test Match.

***

Dismissal (Again)

September 2012

And so it's back to the backbenches for the Member for North West Hampshire. My departure had been widely predicted; bonds in George Young have been yielding over 7% for most of the summer, and my friends in the City tell me that this indicates that exit from whatever Zone you happen to be in is imminent. And so it was.

There have been vivid descriptions of the exchanges between my fellow departing Ministers and the Prime Minister; and I just want to reassure readers that, in my case, there were no protestations, tears or hysterics. Or indeed wine. It is the third time I have left Government - a score of almost Mandelsonian proportions – and I am now familiar with the routine. A few days in the decompression chamber and then back into the real world. And, in any case, there are many excellent and younger colleagues on the backbenches who deserve a turn at the wheel.

The logistics of a Government reshuffle are complex. Although an outgoing Minister will have known for up to a day that he or she is heading for the departure lounge, secrecy is meant to be preserved and the Minister has to remain at his post until his successor arrives. The time of that arrival is not known in advance; nor indeed the identity of the new incumbent; but, once both are known, things move quickly. I had about 15 minutes to get some champagne out of the fridge, share it with my hardworking staff and make a short but sincere valedictory oration of appreciation for their support for the last two and a half years.

I handed over the key to the office; the key to the red box; the key to the sack in which the red box comes; and my pass to Downing Street. I strode out of the Leader's Office with my head held high; and then realised I had nowhere to go. The man for whom I had vacated my office had his office at the Department of Health, where I would not be welcome as they had a new Secretary of State there. The MPs who had newly joined the Government from the backbenches were busy getting briefed in their new Departments. Clearing out their offices in the House to make room for the old sweats would be at the bottom of their priorities. But, until they move out, us old sweats are homeless. I am living out of a cardboard box, working on the edge of my secretary's desk on the perimeter of the Parliamentary precincts, answering by hand the many letters of condolence constituents have been good enough to send.

I telephoned the Whip in charge of accommodation in order to solve the problem and get a proper office. There was no reply. He too had been reshuffled.

***

Backbencher

September 2012

At the beginning of the month, a large rock was pitched into the middle of the Ministerial pond. The reshuffle. There was much turbulence and reports of some distress but, three weeks later, there are but a few ripples left on the surface. Names have been erased from doors on the Ministerial corridor, departmental letter headings have been changed, government drivers re-assigned and party conference programmes reprinted. Those who believe the mythology of "Yes Minister" will assert that the destiny of the country remains unaltered, because Sir Humphrey reigns supreme.

This constitutional issue will remain unaddressed, but life certainly changes for the players involved. Early on Saturday morning, there is no longer a ring at my front door as a Ministerial red box is delivered in a sack, in exchange for an illegible signature on the driver's Blackberry; nor does the box have to be lugged back on the train from Andover to Waterloo on a Monday morning, to the inconvenience of my fellow-travellers. Indeed, the 7.35 can be ditched for a later train and different travelling companions. The mobile phone does not have to be on all the time, in case of some crisis requiring my attention; nor do I have to listen to every news story on a Wednesday in preparation for Business Questions on a Thursday. Nor, in the name of collective responsibility, do I have to defend everything that Ministers may say or do. (They are now spared having to defend what I get up to.)

There have been further compensations. A number of speaking engagements have been removed from my diary – most being taken on by my successor as Leader of the House. Of those that remained, one has been cancelled owing to the difficulty of selling tickets for a dinner addressed by a mere backbencher. I am also spared from being part of the doughnut after the Leader's Speech at the Party Conference in Birmingham, and can watch his oration in comfort on television at home.

There will be a souvenir of my past career; every outgoing Minister is allowed to purchase a red box, (compensating the Treasury for any expenditure incurred.) This will be added to the collection, currently in the attic, of boxes from previous posts.

Of course, there is a downside to all of this. One is no longer near the centre of events. If one pulls a lever, it is no longer connected to the machine. And my wife, who is a keen follower of my career, has spotted that there are less claims on my time. A number of outstanding household chores have been drawn to my attention...

Recall (Again)

November 2012

My retirement was interrupted by a call to arms from the Prime Minister, following Andrew Mitchell's resignation as Chief Whip. After two years of being addressed as "Leader", with all its Teutonic overtones, I was now to be addressed as "Chief", like the head of a Sioux tribe. The column was discontinued as the Chief Whip does not only not speak; he doesn't write either. The following columns were jotted down but never published.

***

Captain's Table

March 2013

One of the privileges of being Chief Whip is that there is a table reserved for you in the Members' Dining Room in the House of Commons. As long as you are the Conservative Chief Whip. The People's Party regards all hungry men and women as equal, and my Opposite Number has no such privilege. The Members' Dining Room observes political apartheid, with the Conservatives at one end, the Labour Party at the other; and the Liberal Democrats in the middle. Right next to the buffet.

At times, when I was eating elsewhere, I sublet my table to other members of the Whips Office, who used the patronage with intelligence. And hopefully for intelligence. On a cruise, you might get asked to the Captain's Table. In parliament, you might get asked to the Chief Whip's Table.

After a vote one evening, I looked into the Dining Room to check that my table at the far end was vacant, and went to the Smoking Room next door to find three guests. Having identified some congenial companions to join me at my table, we went back to the Dining Room. Drama. At the table were two women Labour MPs. They had landed, when my gaze was averted, behind enemy lines and were occupying hostile territory. Space was available for them at the other end of the dining room, but they had chosen to be surrounded by members of the non-People's Party. Chivalry required that the ladies be left to dine in peace; custom required that their peaceful dinner should be elsewhere.

Colleagues at the neighbouring tables stopped eating to see how the Chief – as the Chief Whip is known – would resolve this social dilemma. Would he and his three guests retreat ignominiously, confirming the worst fears about the ability of the Whips Office to exercise discipline? Or would he provoke a confrontation, which would end up within seconds on the social media, confirming the public's impression of the Conservative Party? Some reached for their iPhones in anticipation.

The matter was resolved amicably. The ladies from the People's Party generously offered to move to their side of the lines; and, to compensate them for their disruption and to show that the age of chivalry was not dead, I then sent them a bottle of champagne.

At this point, the issue of moral hazard needs to be raised. A precedent had been set; there was a risk, was there not, that every evening members of the People's Party would occupy the Chief Whip's table? They would sit there, with their tongues hanging out, waiting for the appropriate inducement to sit elsewhere. These are the challenges, amongst others, that I bequeath to my successor.

Seating Arrangements

March 2013

On Budget Day the focus is, rightly, on the Chancellor of the Exchequer. He has spent weeks listening to colleagues, assessing options produced by the Treasury and HMRC, reading OBR forecasts and hearing the views of the Bank of England and international commentators. His task is a substantial one, on which may hang the fortunes of the administration.

The task of the Chief Whip on Budget Day, by contrast, is less daunting but not without its challenges. It is to resolve the question of "placement" on the Front Bench during the Budget Statement.

There is the free market option. Let competition decide; reward those who get up early (alarm clock Britain) and bag a good seat; let those with energy and drive elbow their way up the green bench towards the despatch box, and into the frame of the cameras in the Chamber.

This option involves minimal input from the Chief. But, as an unreformed Keynesian, I recognise that the laissez-faire option may be suboptimal; you might end up with lots of alpha males, and no alpha females; too many LibDems or too few; or some muscular junior Ministers who had no right to be there, but might jump the queue. And, potentially damaging, we could have an unseemly squabble on camera, as seniority was asserted and disputed.

To avoid these outcomes, and to ensure those on the Front Bench could sit in some comfort during the Budget speech, I drew up a seating plan. This required the diplomacy of a society hostess entertaining A list guests who might easily take offence.

I circulated the list after the Budget Cabinet, with apologies to those I had offended. The list had the right percentage of LibDems, women, and an appropriate place for the PM, the Deputy PM and Chief Secretary. My task was assisted by one highly-placed colleague who had just got off an aeroplane. Please could he not be in view, as he was likely to doze off. As the Budget had winners and losers, I wanted to get some winners in the frame.

This leads to my suggestion for the Chancellor and his next Budget. There is not enough room on the Front Bench for every member of the Cabinet and the statutory Whip. But there is a direct relationship between the diameter of a Cabinet Minister and the numbers the Front Bench can accommodate. The thinner, the better.

So let us have an incentive; the winners in the Budget should be those who have slimmed most in the preceding year. Good for the health of the Government, and easier for the Chief Whip.

***

Members' Cloakroom

September 2013

For nearly forty years, I have hung my coat in the Members' Cloakroom from a hanger in the same rack. The exact location of my hanger within the rack has moved marginally. Names are listed alphabetically by surname and I am often last. In my early years, that place was held by George Younger; then later by Richard Younger-Ross; and now by my good friend Nadhim Zahawi, who is unlikely to be challenged for that slot, unless Pinchas Zukerman abandons the violin for a political career. On my other side has hung, for 30 years, the expensive outerwear of Tim Yeo.

In my youth, I hung up a leather motorbike jacket, for that was my form of transport. On top of the rack was my helmet. When the Honda 175 was sold in Labour's years of austerity in the 1970s, I traded down to two wheels without power assistance, and a cloth cap and wind-cheater took over. To be replaced again by a crash helmet when I became Secretary of State for Transport, and it was incorrect to be seen on a bicycle with my head unprotected. And, with my Party back in Government and cutting the cost of politics, I have kept the bicycle and spurned the temptation of a Ministerial limousine.

The lower names in the alphabet hang their coats nearest to the entrance from New Palace Yard. It is therefore convenient as one can disrobe the moment one enters.

Recently, someone has decided to re-arrange the cloakroom, disturbing centuries of tradition. Instead of it being done alphabetically by surname, it is now done alphabetically by constituency. It took me some time to find Hampshire North West, but I found it under North West Hampshire. My new rack is furthest from the entrance – in fact, it is the first one as you leave the precincts.

The new arrangements reinforce the convention that we refer to each other not by name, but by constituency – the Rt Hon Member for North West Hants, (not Sir George Young) - but this is under attack by the modernisers. I suppose it may save the turbulence caused by a by-election, when someone whose name begins with A is replaced by someone whose name begins with W, and everyone moves up. On the other hand, when the boundaries are changed, there will be more turbulence.

There is silver lining in the cloud. There are more racks than MPs, which means that there are a few vacant coathangers at the end of the constituency alphabet.

I therefore continue to leave my crash helmet, bicycle clips and fluorescent jacket where they have been for decades, leaving the North West Hants slot unfilled.

HOUSE OF COMMONS

Name Plates in Members' Cloakroom

The Administration Committee previously agreed that name plates should be organised alphabetically by constituency rather than by name.

Name plates have now been updated using data from the Library's Members' Names Information Service. Members will find their pegs have moved and should look for their full constituency name as stated by the Boundary Commission.

Any personal belongings left in the Cloakroom after the Rise of House on Thursday 18 July have been removed and can be obtained by contacting ████
████████████████████████████████

Tony Benn's Funeral

March 2014

One of the obligations of the Government Chief Whip is to represent the Prime Minister at funerals and memorial services. He or she is the Executive's Mourner-in-Chief, standing respectfully beside the Lord Lieutenant of whichever county will hold the mortal remains of a former colleague.

Thus it was that I was in St Margaret's Church, Westminster at the funeral of Tony Benn. In the same pew with me were the Leader of the Opposition and his wife, and Ed Balls and Yvette Cooper. I was isolated, totally surrounded by my life's political opponents. An island of blue in a sea of red.

Arthur Scargill and Ken Livingstone were but a stone's throw away and, as the service progressed, I could hear in my left ear the rich baritone voice of Jack Straw, sitting directly behind me.

It was a moving service, with memorable tributes to their father by three of Tony Benn's children. He would have been proud of them. As we reached the conclusion, I looked down at the service sheet and there it was on the final page. The People's Hymn. The Red Flag. My blood froze.

It was the ultimate moral dilemma. I had been despatched to represent the Government at the service, and part of the service was the Labour Party's tribal song. Etiquette would require me to join in. Boycotting would have been a discourtesy. But my Party – and my Leader – might regard participation as the ultimate betrayal. "We always thought George was a bit of a leftie – now we know. Singing the Red Flag in public. Can you believe it?" It was like inviting an Arsenal fan to sing "Come on you Spurs".

Everyone around me was singing, and of course they had no need to refer to the service sheet. I did not know the lyrics, and it is strong stuff. For readers similarly unfamiliar with the narrative, the chorus goes as follows:

"Then raise the scarlet standard high.
Within its shade we'll live and die,
Though cowards flinch and traitors sneer,
We'll keep the red flag flying here."
So what did I do? I joined in, trying hard not to flinch or sneer, and observing with relief that there were no cameras to record the event.

My revenge will be sweet. I hope many comrades from the People's Party will overlook my enthusiastic support for the Conservative Party and attend my Memorial Service when the time comes. On the final page of the service sheet will be verses familiar to members of David Cameron's entourage, but less so to the others. The Eton Boating Song. I expect the Brothers to join in. I am only sorry I won't be there to enjoy the spectacle.

St Margaret's Church
Westminster Abbey

The Funeral of

Tony Benn

3rd April 1925 – 14th March 2014

Thursday 27th March 2014

11.00 am

The Right Honourable Tony Benn MP
by
Andrew Tift 1998
© Palace of Westminster

A Departing Gift

June 2014

The engagement with my opposite number – the Chief Whip from Australia – was in the diary, with a note that he would be presenting me with a gift. Anxious to reciprocate, I was about to send out for some House of Commons cufflinks from the Souvenir Shop, when I was told that the advice from Protocol in the Foreign Office was that this was not necessary.

And so my guest, by background a farmer, was ushered in holding a bag in which was a whip. Not a small whip that a jockey might use to motivate his horse, but a 10 foot long Australian Stock Whip with a plaited handle made of kangaroo hide, to which was affixed several thongs of different width, known respectively as the Keeper, the Thong, the Fall and the Cracker - the sort of whip that a lion tamer might have used in Bertram Mills Circus.

I asked him to demonstrate how the whip was used, and was told my room was not big enough for this. Nor was the Whips main office next door. We carried the whip out to a small courtyard below my office, exiting via the Members' Lobby. Some tourists pursed their lips when told by their guide that the gentleman with the menacing thong they had just seen was the Government Chief Whip.

Once in the courtyard, we made sure there were no passers-by who might be injured, and Scott went into action. A sound as of gunfire echoed round the building, and there were screams from a nearby office. I stopped Scott before he went any further, conscious that under the House's security arrangements, there was a risk that everyone would be locked in their rooms while the terrorists were neutralised. We got back without being tasered.

Scott insisted that this was a personal gift to me and not one that should be handed in to the office. In accordance with the Ministerial Code, I instructed my staff to find out what the Whip was worth. Over a certain figure, and I could keep it – no questions asked.

Above a certain sum, if I wanted to keep it, I would have to pay. If I didn't want to pay, it would go to the Government.

Three minutes later, a white faced official came into my office. He apologised. He had been unable to establish the value of the Whip. When he googled this particular brand of whip to establish its market value, all the relevant sites were barred by the Parliamentary authorities as having inappropriate adult content. He logged off before the thought police came round to locate the sado-masochists based in the Houses of Parliament, anxious to pursue some serious flagellation.

After leaving the Government as Chief Whip in July 2014, the column was resumed.

Choosing a Successor

August 2014

I was accosted in Andover a few days ago by a constituent who said how much he enjoyed reading my column in the local paper. I was about to tell him that I hadn't written one for nearly two years, but caught myself in time. If I can be credited with the authorship of readable material without writing anything, why spoil things? Not only could I save myself the trouble of writing a column, but, if I did so, it might not live up to his expectations. So I thanked him for the compliment.

For the past two years, readers of the Advertiser have been spared my fortnightly columns. They stopped on my appointment as Chief Whip. Followers of the House of Cards will know that Chief Whips do not do anything so frivolous as write for the local paper, but instead plot the downfall of their rivals and push people off the top of tall buildings. So the column was suspended and the traditional radio silence of the Chief Whip maintained. I could not possibly have commented.

In the meantime, my parliamentary colleagues from Romsey and Devizes have more than compensated with some refreshing columns of their own, keeping readers informed about what is happening locally and at Westminster. As Chief Whip, I read them to see if there was any trace of unacceptable independence of thought which might destabilise the Government. None was detected.

And so the silence might have continued, had not the Editor written to me on my resignation as Chief Whip last month, suggesting that the column might be disinterred. Which it might be.

Much has happened since I last wrote, including my intention to retire at the next election. This has had a galvanising effect on my local party. Those hoping to inherit the seat have attended local party functions; bought raffle tickets; canvassed in the local elections; run committee rooms on the day and carried out local surveys in Andover High Street. An infusion of young blood swept through the North West Hampshire Conservatives as over a hundred applicants unblocked some of our arteries.

The excellent Kit Malthouse, whose picture I was pleased to see in the paper on August 1st, won the final selection, chaired by my former Parliamentary colleague Matthew Parris, and his name will be on the ballot paper on May 7th 2015.

Following all this activity, the advice from the Party's agent was emphatic. "George, you should retire more often"

***

Holiday in France

August 2014

In France last week for a family holiday, I was reminded how seriously the French take their patriotism. When my father worked in the British Embassy in Paris, he would take me to the England versus France Rugby Match with mixed loyalties. Emotionally, he wanted England to win; but, professionally, he knew that diplomatic relations would freeze if les Anglais defeated the home team on French soil.

Fifty years later, I noticed the dominance of French cars on their roads. Not a Japanese car to be seen. When I remarked on the presence of a Mercedes, I was told it belonged to a German with a second home nearby. If you wanted a hire car, it was likely to be a Citroën or a Renault (though the Satnav has an English speaking option.)

So when we were recommended to go to a nearby open air theatre, we assumed it would be to witness a comedy by Molière or, if we were unlucky, a tragedy by Corneille or Racine - famous, as I recall from my time doing French A levels, for his mastery of the dodecasyllabic Alexandrine. But no, the play was Romeo and Juliet, by Shakespeare. Again, we assumed this would be a translation into French to attract the locals; but no. It was to be in English and with an English cast. Perhaps a consequence of France being in the EU is that they cannot discriminate against British actors who may be better placed than the French to perform Shakespeare in his native tongue. And well performed it was too. True, Juliet had what appeared to be a contemporary tattoo on her left ankle, but then the 15th century Veronese might have been ahead of the game here.

However, French patriotism asserted itself at the end of the visit. Attached to a nearby castle was a Museum of History and Miniatures. In the words of the brochure "The museum awaits you for an original historical visit through stunning sketches which tell key events of world history.....important battles...." And well worth a visit. "Ça vaut le detour" as the French might say.

Pride of place in the museum was a miniature reconstruction of the Battle of Castillon in 1453. I must have been asleep when we covered this seminal encounter when I was at school. A French army, under Jean Bureau, confronted an English army under John Talbot at the end of the Hundred Years' War. Our guide told us that this was also the first battle in European history where the use of cannon was a major factor in determining the victor.

I asked our guide what had been the result. " Malheureusement pour vous, Monsieur, les Anglais ont perdu" he said, with no visible disappointment.

The Portrait

November 2014

I have played my part in many innovative ways of raising funds in North West Hants. Bruce Parker has hosted me on a Desert Island, playing my discs and asking about my career. Aurelia and I have cycled on our tandem, walked a marathon on Watership Down and contributed umpteen recipes for local cookery books. The Hurstbourne Tarrant Development Trust came up with a fresh approach, namely inviting me to sit while my portrait was painted, to help raise funds for their new Community Centre.

Resident artist Tom Coates generously gave up his time to conduct a Master Class at Hurstbourne Tarrant School one evening last week. Some sixty paying customers turned up to see how their MP might be immortalised on canvas.

His Master Class was arranged in such a way that the audience was in front of his easel and I was on a stage behind it. This meant that I couldn't see what he was up to. The respectful silence of the first session was interrupted by a burst of laughter. I had acquired a pair of horns, happily removed from the finished work. As he painted, Tom related anecdotes about his previous sitters, including the late Queen Mother who was anxious to ensure that he was always properly refreshed. The audience asked respectful questions about his technique, as the blank canvas became populated with the recognisable features of the local MP.

I asked Tom what was the difference between a photograph and a portrait. "Magic" was his answer.

I asked if his magic might give me a little more hair and a little less paunch, and he replied that magic was expensive. Artistic integrity is clearly important to him. A previous sitter had apparently enquired whether her bust might be enhanced and received a similar reply.

I make two apologies. First, to Tom. Your jokes were funny, and I am conscious I was the only person not to laugh at them. This is because I was focussed on maintaining the same facial expression throughout the sitting. Second, to the lady sitting three in from the left in the back row. You may not have been stared at unblinkingly for two hours before by a man with a leer. But the reason is as previously stated, to keep my head pointing in the same direction throughout.

After two hours, the masterpiece was pronounced complete, to spontaneous applause.

I ended the evening full of admiration for professional models. They have to sit still for a lot longer; and often without the benefit of several layers of clothing.

Clearing Out

December 2014

We should all make a will, we are repeatedly told in the Money Section of our newspapers. Failure to do so may mean that insensitive decisions are taken about one's assets, according to some rigid formula set out by Parliament for which I bear some responsibility. This may cause resentment amongst relatives, whose expectations are dashed. True, we will no longer be there to witness this distress, but it is not how we wish to be remembered. "Loving Husband and Father, who messed up by not making a Will." So I have a will, and the only complication is that I can't remember who the executors are and they may predecease me.

A similar requirement about the disposal of assets has arrived on my desk at Westminster, entitled Dissolution Arrangements. These are not measures that are required for Members of Parliament who are dissolute – for which sanctions are already available - but arrangements that kick in when Parliament is dissolved, as it must be by the end of March next year. Assets acquired at public expense must, rightly, be accounted for and data about one's constituents properly safeguarded.

This would have been simpler had I retired at the end of my first Parliament in 1974. The only assets in the office were a typewriter and a filing cabinet. Both were my own, as there was no facility for equipping MPs at public expense at that time. Since then, much has changed and hardware has been showered on MPs to enable them to discharge their duties more effectively. This must now be tracked down and accounted for.

In reading the instructions about the disposal of these assets, in advance of my parliamentary demise, I came across a facility I had never heard of. "It is recommended that the records held by your office, including those held off-site in the Iron Mountain facility should be reviewed." The Iron Mountain. A feature of the Parliamentary landscape that I had not encountered in 40 years there. The accompanying instructions are pretty grim.

All websites must be disclaimed; security passes to Parliament will be de-activated; email access to the parliamentary account denied; cars must be removed from the underground car park – (no mention of bicycles); all our rooms in Portcullis House will be locked; the Message Bureau will take no more messages; PCs must not be taken off the estate; MP's biography pages will be removed from the Parliamentary website; all Voicemail will be deactivated; House of Commons stationery and envelopes must be locked away; and all IT equipment must be returned.

By comparison, making a will and dying is a doddle.

***

Twitching Curtains

December 2014

May I, for the last time as your local MP, send to all readers of the Advertiser my very best wishes for 2015 – for which the prospects look better than many recent years.

Thanks to the Fixed Term Parliament Act 2011, we know there will be a General Election on May 7th. Some commentators believe there will be two elections next year - which may not be on every reader's wish list. So convinced was one News Channel that we are in for a double election that they went through their records to find out the last time this happened, which was in 1974. They then went through their records again to see if anyone who was around then was still around now. The answer was that there are ten MPs in the House of Commons who fought both elections in that year who are still in the

House today. One was to be invited on their Sunday morning politics show to reminisce.

On Friday, I got the call. Would I go to London to take part in this studio discussion? I declined. Giving up half a day for 15 minutes on television is something I would have leapt at in 1974, with a second election in my marginal seat imminent. But with no direct personal stake in next year's election, this was on the wrong side of my indifference curve. (I do of course have an enormous interest in the victory of my successor, the excellent Kit Malthouse, for whom all stops will be pulled out.)

But so keen were they to know my views that, when I declined to go to London to broadcast, they offered to send a crew to my home near Andover. And so it came to pass.

Normally, when an Outside Broadcasting Unit draws up outside the home of a Tory backbencher on a Sunday, it is because a tabloid has published some infelicity about his private life. So there was a little curtain twitching in the village when the van with the huge dish on the roof drew up. The best way for my neighbours to find out what their MP had got up to was to watch the appropriate channel, which many did.

They may have been disappointed, if not surprised, to hear their local MP talking about constitutional reform. As I informed the nation about the operation of the Fixed Term Parliament Act of 2011, and it became clear that there was nothing salacious to savour, so they returned to wrapping up their Christmas presents.

House of Cards

January 2015

One of my Christmas gifts, from a thoughtful son, was the DVD of the House of Cards – an American remake of the original book and then TV serial by Michael (now Lord) Dobbs. Both chronicle the activities of a Chief Whip, the original serial being located in the House of Commons while the remake crosses the Atlantic to the House of Representatives.

The box set came with a warning on its side – "Suitable only for persons of 18 years and over. Very strong language, sex, sexual fetish, hard drug use, suicide references."

This sounded different from my experience of the job as Chief Whip from 2012 to 2014, even allowing for some poetic licence. Clearly, they do things differently in the States.

In the British version, the Chief Whip's name is Francis Urquhart. The Americans have renamed him Francis Underwood, perhaps because when the Pilgrim Fathers arrived in 1620, there wasn't an Urquhart on board and so the name doesn't resonate there. But it was important that Francis' surname began with a U, so he could wear his F U cufflinks.

I happened to have seen the first episode two years ago, when Netflix launched the US series to subscribers in London. I met Michael Dobbs and Kevin Spacey, who plays Francis Underwood, and expressed surprise that the many boring meetings it was my job to attend as Chief Whip never featured in their scripts; and that Francis won all his arguments and for ever came out on top, whereas my experience was that the Chief Whip carried the can when anything went wrong.

I have so far watched 14 of the 26 episodes. In these, the Chief Whip has persuaded the police to drop criminal charges against an ally, trashed a public building with some drunken friends, denounced the Almighty, had an adulterous affair with a journalist and double-crossed just about everyone who has come his way. Oh, and committed two murders. (Episode 26, when I reach it, may deliver his well-deserved come-uppance.)

This portrayal does a serious injury to the reputation of a noble profession, albeit back in 1868 the Northern Star wrote "Now in the popular mind, the office of whip is one with which many strange fancies and doubts are associated and one, too which all combine to a suspicion to render mysterious."

So here is a challenge to any ambitious dramatist. Put the record straight. I commission you to write a 26 episode serial about a Chief Whip who is sober, monogamous, God-fearing, discreet, loyal to his friends and to his leader, and averse to homicide. But don't expect to get rich.

***

Last Word

March 2015

In four weeks time, we have the dissolution of Parliament, so, along with 649 other MPs, I am dissolved with it. As I am not returning, this means evacuating my office in the House of Commons so the next incumbent has vacant possession. After 41 years, this inevitably means that there is an accumulation of items which either need to be discarded or packaged up. The two Ministerial red boxes will be kept – to join five others in the attic at home – and the pictures by local artists will be repatriated home to Hampshire. Most of the books will be donated to charities, and the various awards I have won will be scrutinised by my wife before they are allowed on to the mantelpiece at home.

Then there are all the files – box after box after box. Most of the contents will be shredded but an exchange of correspondence nearly 20 years ago, when I was in the Cabinet as Secretary of State for

Transport, caught my eye and I think it should be preserved for posterity.

One of our political weekly magazines, the Spectator, published a series of paid-for advertisements for gentleman's clothing, each of which featured a cartoon of a member of the Cabinet promoting the outfitter's wares. In the week in which I disposed of the country's holding of the shares in Railtrack, I was featured in front of a row of suits with the caption "Don't miss the great rail sale."

My wife contacted Aquascutum to gently enquire why, without his consent, they were using her husband to promote their products. This generated the following letter.

"Dear Lady Young,

Further to our telephone conversations, I am pleased to confirm that Aquascutum are delighted to offer Sir George Young a suit in recognition of his assistance in our Spectator cartoon campaign."

I was despatched to Regent Street to be measured for this compensatory suit, and it occurred to me that this might constitute a gift to be entered in the Register of Members' Interests.

I made contact with the Parliamentary Commissioner for Standards to seek guidance, and then wrote to Aquascutum.

"I have been in touch with the Parliamentary Commissioner for Standards, in connection with the generous gift of a suit from Aquascutum. It appears that I will have to register the suit as payment in kind for appearing as a model in the Company's catalogue. As I am not particularly anxious to do this, I would be grateful if you would send me an invoice for the suit, so there will have been no gift."

Eventually an invoice arrived "Chichester SB. Suit Size 42 Lng. Sage Red. £495." A cheque was despatched by return, with a photocopy retained, to avoid an entry in the Register which would have caused some amusement in the media.

And the suit still fits.

don't miss
the great rail sale!